EMPOWERED FOR 1
YEARS OF YOUR LIFE

50+

THE EMERGING

JOSHUA & CALEB

GENERATION

JOHN BONECK

THE EMERGING

JOSHUA & CALEB

GENERATION

DEDICATION

To those who have gone before and paved the way.

ACKNOWLEDGEMENTS

Patti and Phil Lutz for shared vision and love. Trudy Goerk for her poetic legacy. MorningStar 50+ Blessing Generation for walking out God's calling. Rick and Dave and the entire MorningStar Ministries staff for who they are and how they serve and love.

TABLE OF CONTENTS

OPENING

*I will go in the strength of the L*ORD *God; I will make mention of Your righteousness, of Yours only. O God, You have taught me from my youth; and to this day I declare Your wondrous works. Now also when I am old and grayheaded, O God, do not forsake me, until I declare Your strength to this generation, Your power to everyone who is to come. (Ps 71:16-18)*

By the time you enter the second half-century of your life, you have walked through a lot, both good and bad, just as David did when he penned Psalm 71. You've experienced things you loved and things you wish you never had encountered. You've done things you are pleased with and things you are sorry for. Yes, you are like every other 50+er.

But unlike many others, you will live the rest of your life in a greater measure of fullness and satisfaction than you thought possible. You are not finished. You are not excluded. The fullness of time has converged with your years of experience, positioning you to take your rightful place in God's great plan for you, walking in your calling.

This book is meant to activate you to live with greater

joy and fulfillment than ever before—because you have finally arrived at this key time in your life for which God has been preparing you. What is ahead is God's great plan for your life in the coming days.

God is calling you, "the Joshua and Caleb generation," to take your place. You are an extremely important part of God's plan for this crucial time in which we live. You are "complete in Him" as Colossians 2:10 says. You will live your days with loving intentionality and will also be able to lead and love others into their future, a future that God desires for all His children.

Section 1, "Activating God's Purposes," defines our calling and addresses areas that might be holding us back from walking into our destiny. The Holy Spirit will do the work to heal possible troubling areas and wounds.

Section 2, "Applying God's Purposes," will help you walk out the best years of your life in fulfillment as well as equip you with practical tools that will make a difference in many others' lives.

Section 1:

ACTIVATING GOD'S PURPOSES

THE PRESENT-DAY
JOSHUAS AND CALEBS

*Be strong and of good courage; do not be dismayed, for the
LORD your God is with you wherever you go. (Josh 1:9)*

It's happening again. As it was with Joshua and Caleb,
"older" ones in the faith are leading and blessing the
generation below them. 50+ers in the ministry room
are speaking blessings to the younger generation. Younger
people around us 50+ers are weeping. A few are physically
shaking. They're thanking and hugging us. Us, of all people, a group of 50+ers just wanting to walk in the fullness of
God's calling.

Finally, the woman whom my teammate and I have been
blessing is composed enough to explain. "I've been a pastor
for years," she says. "I bless the people in my church all the
time. I keep giving out." Her voice catches in her throat as
she continues, "But no one has ever blessed me." My 50+
teammate and I see the total change. It's like she's finally
being accepted into the family. She feels at home. God is
touching her in a way only a loving Father can. We have just
declared a generational blessing over her from a father and
a mother in the Lord.

A few years earlier most of us wouldn't have believed it possible. But God changed all of that. Now a group of us "mature adults" is having spiritual fun again at the conference. We're declaring generational blessings and are feeling God's affirmation and energy in our lives even as we continue for a full three hours, individually blessing about 200 of all ages.

Our time has come. It's really happening. It's almost too hard to believe. And we're connecting with the younger generation. They'll never reach their potential on their own. They need us. And they know it and want it.

We're connecting with each other as 50+ers, too. We are praying with each other. We are worshipping with each other. We share things with each other that only those our age can understand. We are seeing God do things.

We're even having some fun times together. Jokes come easily. We're relaxed around each other.

No, this isn't happening in a "senior center." It's happening in our church. We're not retiring. We're refiring.

Sound too good to be true? If I wasn't experiencing it, I'd say the same thing.

It's a new day. The old rules are thrown out.

It's God and His timing. He's calling us, all of us, to enter the fullness of our lives right now, not just at our church, but everywhere we 50+ers live. He isn't finished with us. He's renewing us. He's using us as part of his Harvest company. We, his sons and daughters, are being called right now.

We're in churches all over America. We're saying, "God gave us promises. We're not finished yet. We have a purpose. We will fulfill our calling."

And we're right.

We're 50+ers--known as the "baby boomer" generation. Some of us were born even earlier. God's time for us is now, and He is ready to take us on an exciting adventure. He has equipped us uniquely for it. We are stepping into our destiny--and are a modern-day parallel to Joshua and Caleb.

You know their story. Much of it is told in Numbers 13 and 14. Moses chooses a leader from each of the 12 tribes to spy out the land of Canaan and bring back a report.

The spies return and declare it to be a land that "truly flows with milk and honey." They even bring back fruit as evidence. "Nevertheless," they say, "the people who dwell in the land are strong; the cities are fortified and very large; moreover we saw the descendants of Anak there."

Then Caleb speaks up, "Let us go up at once and take possession, for we are well able to overcome it."

To which the naysayers retort, "We are not able to go up against the people, for they are stronger than we.... There we saw the giants (the descendants of Anak came from the giants); and we were like grasshoppers in our own sight."

Joshua and Caleb tear their clothes and continue the plea to take the land. They say to the Israelites, "Do not rebel against the LORD, nor fear the people of the land, for they are our bread."

The congregation responds by trying to stone Joshua and Caleb, that is, until the glory of the LORD appears in the tabernacle of meeting and drastically changes the order of the conversation.

God asks Moses, "How long will these people reject Me? And how long will they not believe Me, with all the signs which I have performed among them?" God punishes the people, actually killing the other ten spies and many others with the plague, and declaring that those people 20 years and older will die in the wilderness over the next 40 years and never enter the Promised Land.

But Joshua and Caleb, who believe God, are spared. God promises them that they will enter the Promised Land. God says, "But of My servant Caleb, because he has a different spirit in him and has followed Me fully, I will bring into the land where he went, and his descendants shall inherit it."

Many of us 50+ers today are like Joshua and Caleb, having seen God's glory and miraculous signs and placing our trust in Him. Some of us were ignited by the Holy Spirit during the Jesus revolution of the '60s and '70s. Others were changed by the Holy Spirit in the Charismatic Movement or the Catholic Renewal. Still others of us read one of Rick Joyner's books or another inspired book, and our hearts were stirred and changed. Our spiritual lives began with an encounter with God, launching our love for Him.

We are full of faith for what God can do, just as Joshua and Caleb were. They loved God and declared that with God's help they could conquer God's enemies and enter the Promised Land. God loves their hearts and gives them promises.

Now here's a big thing. Though God gives promises to Joshua and Caleb, it takes 40 years for the promises to be fulfilled. Forty years. Joshua and Caleb can't just run back into the Promised Land. They have to walk through the wilderness with the rest of the Israelites day after day after day. They have to eat the same food morning and evening. They have to watch as relatives and others their age die off. They have to live with an unbelieving group of people. We also have to walk with some brothers and sisters who don't understand. We also have personal anguish when others will not also believe God's good report.

During those wilderness years God matures Joshua and Caleb. Joshua spends much of his time in the tabernacle of meeting as Moses' assistant. He understands God's presence. Caleb leads his family and cares for his offspring.

Much of what we have encountered over the years hasn't been easy either. But we still love God with all our hearts. He has placed promises in our hearts, too. We know there is more for us. We hope or sense we could be entering the most significant time in our lives. Even if we've walked through wilderness experiences, we will not die in the wilderness. Though the cultural church around us has been faltering for years, we're not going to.

So here we are today--just like Joshua and Caleb after

40 long years in the wilderness. The fullness of time has occurred on God's clock.

Joshua and Caleb are in their 80s when they get to the border of their Promised Land. They, however, are not going to pass the baton on to the next generation and go play golf. Oh, no, not after what they've been through. They're seasoned. They're wise. And God's Spirit is on them. Exploits await.

God calls Joshua to lead the next generation into the Promised Land. God declares to Joshua, "I will not leave you nor forsake you.... Be strong and of good courage; do not be dismayed, for the LORD your God is with you wherever you go." (Josh 1:5,9) That next generation can't make it on their own. They need a wise old (let's say, "mature") person who really hears from God, who understands battle and strategy, "a man in whom is the Spirit," as Numbers 27:18 describes.

The younger generation needs us, too. We are called to be their covering. They can't make it to God's promised land without us. We 50+ers, both men and women, are the mature Joshua and Caleb generation. It's "thy Kingdom come" time, and we are to lead the next generation into kingdom life.

And what about Caleb? He is the other half of the Joshua and Caleb generation.

As the head of his family, Caleb helps Joshua in the battle for the Promised Land. Then, after 5 years, he claims God's personal promise for him and his family.

He speaks to Joshua and says,

Here I am this day, eighty-five years old. As yet I am as strong this day as on the day that Moses sent me; just as my strength was then, so now is my strength for war, both for going out and for coming in. Now therefore, give me this mountain of which the LORD spoke in that day; for you heard in that day how the Anakim were there, and

that the cities were great and fortified. It may be that the
Lord will be with me, and I shall be able to drive them out
as the Lord said. (Josh 14:10-12)

Joshua blesses him and gives him Hebron. What a unique place. Joshua 14:14-15 describes it: "Hebron therefore became the inheritance of Caleb the son of Jephunneh the Kenizzite to this day, because he wholly followed the Lord God of Israel. And the name of Hebron formerly was Kirjath Arba (Arba was the greatest man among the Anakim). Then the land had peace."

Did you catch that? Caleb gets to own the city of the biggest giant out there. These are the same giants that 45 years earlier the doubting spies thought were so big that they themselves looked like grasshoppers in comparison. But Caleb had said, "They are our bread." He goes to Hebron and drives out the three children of Anak. Caleb's prophetic words from 45 years earlier are fulfilled.

Many from our current mature Joshua and Caleb generation are also going to "own the city" of what others thought were life's biggest threats.

Hebron has another prophetic characteristic as well. A few years later the Lord speaks to Joshua, telling him to have the children of Israel select "cities of refuge." If a person accidently kills someone, that person can flee there to declare his case "in the hearing of the elders of that city. They shall take him into the city as one of them, and give him a place, that he may dwell among them." (Josh 20:4) Hebron becomes one of those cities. What a great choice. A mature elder lives there. God can count on Caleb to act righteously and wisely. The present-day Calebs are the same.

That's not all. Hebron also becomes a city of the Levites. The very center of Caleb's inheritance is a home to the spiritual life of Israel.

Caleb lives to pass on his inheritance to his children. The present-day Joshuas and Calebs will do the same. We are called to cover the younger generation and lead them into their kingdom inheritance. We are called to train them in spiritual warfare. We are called to be elders in the gate and a protection for those who seek refuge. We are called to live with the Spirit of the LORD at the center of our lives.

We are the matured Joshua and Caleb generation, walking out our destinies, doing exploits.

Really, now, doesn't it sound exciting to be a Joshua or Caleb?

SHAKING OFF THE "WILDERNESS YEARS"

If anyone is in Christ, he is a new creation; old things have passed away; behold, all things have become new. (2 Cor 5:17-18)

I'm sitting at a table with five MorningStar University students. We're sharing lunch together and having a healthy conversation. The topic at the moment is the importance of having the generations in the Lord connected to each other. I mention that many from the 50+ generation have been hurt in the church and don't really see or walk in the fullness of what God has for them.

Andrew, one of the students, quickly jumps in. "That's just like my grandfather," he says. "He used to sing in the choir and in a men's group. He loved music and gospel quartets. But then he became hurt." Andrew continues. "The church he went to was pretty legalistic, I think. Anyway, he missed church a couple weeks and was confronted by one of the church elders. 'You're going to get throat cancer if you don't return to the choir and keep singing,' he told my grandfather.

"Since then my grandfather has never returned to church, and that was many years ago."

I talk with Andrew about what he can do to help his grandfather's wound heal. At the end of our conversation we all pray for Andrew and how he is going to love his grandfather out from under the deep wound he is carrying.

The story of Andrew's grandfather, while sad, is not uncommon. 50+ers have taken many hits and suffered many wounds both inside and outside the church walls over the years.

The pressures of life have a way of wearing us down. Our resilience may not seem to be what it once was. The death of loved ones puts us more in touch with the brevity of life. Our choices become more conservative. We take fewer risks.

And the tragedy is that many Christians who are in their second half-century often believe their usefulness is diminishing (as if working 50 hours a week was the real measuring stick of what made someone useful). They may mainly focus on their grandchildren now, resigned to living a retired life.

But what if God had a surprise for us? What if God spoke to us again and said, "You are still my creation. I am removing the old things from your life. I am making all things new for you"?

That is what He is saying although it may be hard to believe. Society has programmed many 50+ers into believing that their best years are behind, that life on the golf course is the primary option for the years ahead. Society has said that those in their sixties should retire (at least when economically feasible). Many Christians of retirement age have believed society's lie that their "useful" life is over and that all that's left is to retire from active involvement in society. And I believe the enemy of our souls also works to minimize the influence of 50+ers in becoming Joshuas and Calebs to the upcoming generation.

Those of us born in America at the end of World War 2 or shortly after participated in the growth of the mightiest and wealthiest nation in the history of the world. The transformation from a rural to an urban and suburban nation was complete. We went from railroads to interstates to space travel and from telephone to Internet to tweeting. Our stores changed from mom-and-pop owned to Wal-Mart. Our locally-owned banks were bought out by international conglomerates.

During this time we Christians experienced some mighty revivals and outpourings of the Spirit such as the Charismatic and Catholic renewals. We followed Oral Roberts, Katherine Kuhlman, and other great healing evangelists. We witnessed Billy Graham's astounding crusades.

But along the way stuff happened. Marriages began to fall apart, inside the church as well as in the rest of society. Christians got hurt in the church. Success became a god in American life. Keeping up with the Joneses was an acceptable goal. The art of parenting faded. Television, the media, Hollywood, and the Internet replaced parents as the source of truth and understanding. Christian leaders became examples of great moral failure. The organized church often seemed to get sucked into society's whirlpool of moral collapse.

When society declined, much of the organized church did not have the strength or determination to reverse the trend. Instead, many churches began to reflect the culture, ending up with a cultural Christianity that lacked spiritual power.

Other churches hunkered down, keeping their focus on themselves to protect themselves and their children from the evils outside the church.

Still other churches separated themselves from surrounding society, hoping the rapture would take them out of this increasingly worldly mess. And when much of the organized church did that, society had no moral light to guide it and became immoral even more quickly.

At times, too, denominational Christianity often did not allow Christians to walk in their strengths, giftings, and callings. Instead, they had to fit within the prescribed cultural structure of the church. Consequently, many mature Christians functioned meaningfully outside the church system. They were disappointed that they did not have spiritual support from church leadership. I know people who on their own have ministered to single moms, have had their own cell groups, have mentored younger men or women, have been Godly examples in their business lives, have loved senior citizens at rest homes, have cared for anyone they knew who was hurting in some way, etc., etc. Yet, within the church system itself, they did not have an outlet because of the system's restrictions or structure.

Despite cultural Christianity and the moral quagmire that sapped our nation, millions of us in the 50+ generation loved God and worked at bringing up our children in Godly households. We surrendered ourselves to the Holy Spirit's leading and felt God's sustaining hand. We saw God move in miraculous ways in people's lives. We hungered and thirsted after righteousness. We served God and recognized His Lordship in our lives. That we survived and actually have spiritual vitality left may be a minor miracle in itself for many of us. I think Joshua and Caleb encountered a similar culture as they trudged through the desert with them for forty years.

Many 50+ers gave themselves to God and worked within the church structure in fulfilling ways, loving God and ministering to others. We were Sunday school teachers and church board members. We sang in the choir and were active in cell groups. We helped less fortunate people and hurting people in and outside the church.

We have survived through the good and the bad.

Now many 50+ers see their church focusing on the

younger generation as its hope. They hear that the future of the church is the emerging generation. Pastors tell their congregations to get involved in church life, but many 50+ers don't know how to do that. They've already been Sunday school teachers and on mission trips. But now, they don't have the stamina or energy or desire to do what they did when they were younger. They have matured in the LORD and grown in wisdom and understanding but cannot find personal fulfillment in a church that sees the younger generation as its only hope.

The 50+ers are in their second half-century, and the places they served have somehow been transferred to a younger generation. They are now relegated to the sidelines in the same way society transfers retirees to the golf course. Many mature Christians in their 50s or 60s or more now ask, "Is God through with me? What am I to do?"

The cultural church, like society, often treats its mature seniors as less capable of carrying the heavy load, and thus the seniors sit on the sidelines. Neither the cultural church nor society recognizes the latent, but real, power and wisdom that 50+ers have finally attained through age, experience, maturity, and surrender to God.

We 50+ers often feel like spiritual orphans, wanting to fit in but not feeling accepted.

As if age discrimination isn't enough, the church often disqualifies some of its mature members for another reason—the 50+ers were less than perfect in some decisions in the past.

All Christians have walked through experiences that were less than positive. Some have experienced divorce; some have children who are not yet serving the Lord; some have made major errors. When we come to this stage of our lives, we may not even consider that we are qualified for greater things because of some of what we did in the past. And, there are many "Job's comforters" who will be willing to confirm that we are not qualified. Many other Christians willingly write off those who are older, especially if they haven't lived a perfect life.

But what does the Bible say about us? Well, some of the examples from the Word paint a much different picture of qualifications. Take Moses, for example. As an Israelite, he was one of God's chosen people. But he became a murderer when he was 40, having to flee his family and friends and all that he held dear. He spent the next 40 years just making it through life. Then, when he was 80, he encountered a burning bush and God. Despite breaking what would later be one of the Ten Commandments, God used him to lead the Israelites out of bondage and to the Promised Land.

Then there was King David whose male eyes focused on a bathing beauty on a rooftop. Welcome to pornography, b.c. style. He committed adultery with her and actually had her husband killed. Today's church would have disassociated itself from him, especially because it recognized that God had used him earlier in his life but that he had now stumbled, embarrassing the church and, in their thinking, God himself. But God didn't do to David what the modern church might have done. Although David suffered consequences because of his sinful act, he was not banished from God's presence and purpose. From David's marriage that had begun in an adulterous act came a lineage that includes our Savior.

And we know how God blessed David and eventually gave him rest from all his enemies. He even had enough wealth to create the building resources for the Temple that his son Solomon would build.

If you think you are not qualified because of some things you have done, then you do not understand how much your Father loves you. He doesn't remove you because you've sinned or made foolish decisions. He loves you so much that He sent His beloved Son to be a substitute for your sins, allowing you to rise above earthly error and take on a heavenly calling and relationship at every stage of your life.

As a matter of fact, all that you've experienced, both good and bad, has now qualified you for the great calling and purpose in your life in the years ahead—and at one of the most crucial moments in history.

In the business world, employers always look at the prospective employees' qualifications to see whether they will be an appropriate fit for the job opening. God has done the same with you. He sees all you've done and declares that you have grown in wisdom and understanding. He says you are hired for this extremely important position that will change many lives.

You may feel marginalized because of your age or disqualified because you haven't been perfect. But that isn't how God feels. He says, "Old things have passed away; behold, all things are become new."

Something big is coming, and 50+ers are an integral part of it. You as a 50+er are being called to walk out the rest of your life in a profound calling and purpose that you hadn't imagined possible. Nothing can stop you--not society, not cultural Christianity, not Job's comforters, not insecurities, not decreased stamina, not relatives.

Now it's up to us to step into the future God has prepared for us. And one of the first steps is to remove the wounds of the past.

Almost every long-time Christian who is 50 or more has been hurt or wounded in the church. We were rejected for some reason or judged falsely or misunderstood or removed from a position because of doctrinal differences. We may have been part of a church split; we were hurt when a church leader sinned. And on and on into even more serious scenarios.

Consequently, it is sometimes hard for some of us older Christians to deeply trust other Christians and walk in close communion. It is hard to walk in freedom when we ourselves are wounded or broken in some way.

None of us makes it this far without suffering what an

older Christian song called "troubles and trials." We've had some painful experiences in what I call the "wilderness years."

At times we may have tried to cover deep or embarrassing wounds rather than being healed. At other times we didn't realize that wounds still residing in our subconscious continue to impact our present relationships and viewpoint, destroying hope and joy.

Some of us, too, were wounded in the church because we had a wrong understanding of the church of Jesus Christ. Thus, knowing God is calling us into new authority and purpose and being able to walk in the fullness of a calling may be two different things.

I know that was my story for many years. I was fortunate enough to grow up in a strong Christian family. We attended church Sunday morning, Sunday evening, Wednesday night for prayer meeting, and, of course, for any revival when the traveling evangelists would come to our church. Much of my social life was also tied to the church.

My father died of cancer when I was 12, and the men of the church became like surrogate fathers to me. The church continued to be a focal point of my life. When I was in my late 20s, attending graduate school in Colorado, the Holy Spirit revealed His precious presence, and my wife Barb and I became part of the early Charismatic renewal.

We moved to California where I continued my high school teaching career. Naturally, I was heavily involved in the church. I taught the adult Sunday school class, led morning worship, was on the church board, and even served as Sunday school superintendent for a while. Yes, church was important to me. The pastor even called me his "Timothy."

I never should have answered the phone the day the pastor's wife called and put an end to my idyllic church life. Barb and I had traveled back East during summer vacation with our baby son to show him off to the grandparents. When we returned to California, I heard that the pastor's son was about to get married. I was surprised because the pastor's son had some serious personal issues. I called the youth pastor to confirm what I had heard. That was a mistake. He told the pastor that I was questioning the coming marriage.

Within minutes the pastor's wife was on the phone with me, telling me how bad I was, how unspiritual I was, how ashamed I should be for speaking about her son. And on and on. I was crying and trying to defend myself. My world was being destroyed as she kept up, seemingly forever. Her words were cutting my heart and wounding me deeply.

It took several years for that deep hurt to pass. In time I came to realize that the pastor's wife was only acting as a protective mother over her precious son. She would do all she could to protect him. And I honestly forgave her in my heart.

But the wound didn't heal--although I didn't know it. As my professional career developed, my family and I moved around the nation. We attended and fit in churches wherever we moved. However, life was not the same. I was often less engaged in the churches, although I loved the Lord and I loved people.

I wanted to do things for the Lord, but it seemed my efforts were more inspired by my desires and need for recognition than by the Holy Spirit. The big things I tried to do for the Lord just didn't get off the ground. I couldn't figure out why. Despite all of this, I did continue to grow in the Lord. I studied the Word, loved my wife, and continued in my sense of "normal."

Later in life I decided to leave my professional life, go back to graduate school for another degree, and start yet another career. One morning as I was sitting in my living room, reading the Bible and praying before going to class, God the Father came up behind me, reached around the chair, and gave me a squeeze. Yes, I said God the Father hugged me.

In an instant, new revelation flowed into me, and it kept unpacking as I thought about what had just happened. For the first time in my life, I had a personal recognition that God the Father loved me. In an instant God the Father had removed my false identity. I am the child of a loving Father. I exist to love Him back and live a Kingdom life. I care what He, not those around me, thinks.

In childhood I had sung, "Jesus loves me, this I know," but had never had the same sense about my Heavenly Father. I saw God as holy and just. I could even sing "Holy, Holy, Holy" with great sincerity. But a loving Father who personally loved me and was concerned about every little thing I did? It had never entered my mind.

Then I began understanding why.

The church had become my father figure in a strange sort of way after my father died. I served the church, found my identity in the church, and sought acceptance and recognition by the church. Thus, I was devastated when the pastor's wife, an integral part of my "parent" church, rejected me.

For thirty years I had unconsciously carried a wound. When I felt the Father's hug, that wound was healed. I could now be a member of the church family, the body of Christ, without needing to be recognized. What freedom that brought. What peace. He, not the church, is my Source. Now I can truly love the rest of the body of Christ.

My personal example may sound unusual, but many long-time Christians can tell stories of broken relationships or hurts from church life. And, sadly, some of the wounds still fester under just the right recurring circumstances. I've seen it in too many eyes when I've counseled people.

Just as the Father wanted to heal my wound, He wants to heal the wounds of every 50+er.

The Word says, "I can do all things through Christ who strengthens me." An important step, as we already know, is to accept what God's Word says about us.

One of the "all things through Christ" we can do is to open ourselves to the Holy Spirit's healing power. Recognize that any wound is not "normal"--it is not to remain, even if we've had it for years. It is to be healed.

The easier thing might be to say that our hurts are the church's fault or someone else's fault. However, saying that will not remove the brokenness and may actually just make it worse. People in the church (the rest of the body of Christ) are just trying to walk in the revelation of God that they have. They may even be like some of the Israelites who died on the way to the Promised Land. Sometimes in our incomplete understanding, we hurt each other. And when we layer cultural or socio-economic or racial differences and judgments on top of our incomplete understanding, we compound the problem.

When God heals our wounds, we won't be at the mercy of what others say (or what we think they say) about us. If someone in the church mistreats or misjudges us, we no longer get quickly offended or hurt. There is no place for the bad or evil remark to land.

When dealing with wounds from the church or religion, Christians sometimes find it hard to be objective. In the counseling I have done with people, I noticed repeatedly that it is easy for a person to see the other person's faults but hard to recognize that they themselves may also have been partially responsible for the problems.

No matter who's responsible for the wound, it has to be healed. Our great calling for future years is ahead of us, but until we let go of past hurts in our lives, we may not understand or see the plan. The past will continue to dominate our outlooks, attitudes, and actions.

I know most older Christians have forgiven those in the church who hurt them and even have perspective on why the hurts took place. However, there may be some patterns or ways of thinking that are still distorted because of what happened in the past. The good news in all this is that the

Holy Spirit will reveal areas of brokenness He wants to heal as we consciously open ourselves to His voice.

When we surrender our wound to the Holy Spirit, we may have a remaining scar that reminds us of the battle we won, but we will not ache anymore as we did when the wound was still sensitive. Truly, "old things have passed away; behold, all things have become new." A new freedom is ours.

Of course, the church is not the only place we can be wounded. Marriage relationships, parent-child relationships, and other deeply personal connections are all prime areas for wounds to occur. It's just that being wounded in the church or by other Christians seems to create such a distortion of God's real love.

Much evil exists in the world, too, and many Christians have been the victims. We all know individuals who have been abused and seriously mistreated. I do not want to minimize the impact of the violation that occurred to their body and mind. But I know the Healer, who forgave those who crucified Him, will give us the power to grant forgiveness and thus be healed. He wants us to live as a son or daughter in the Kingdom and not as a victim. We are to lead the way into the Promised Land, not die in the wilderness. It often takes others to come along side us to help the healing process if we have been abused. God prepares special people for this healing work.

We humans can be a fragile lot. We can be wounded in a variety of ways. Let me use an example from my wife Barb's life to make the point. At my age, I could use many examples, but this one is easy to explain.

Barb and I had been married for about twelve years and were living in the height of the days of the Charismatic renewal, flowing with what God wanted in our lives. We had moved from California to Harrison, Arkansas, where I became the editor of a Christian book publishing company.

Our child Carson was about five years old, and our marriage was very solid.

But Barb had a personal issue. She saw herself as less than beautiful. Of course, I didn't understand what she was saying. I thought she was as beautiful as a woman could be. However, she would look in the mirror and mention the acne scars and imperfections. I couldn't even see what she was talking about. She finally tried to resolve her facial imperfections by having a medical treatment called a dermabrasion. After the procedure was completed and the skin finally healed, Barb felt better about her appearance. But the issue of her beauty did not disappear.

One day as she was reading her Bible and praying, the Holy Spirit flashed a memory into her mind. She recalled when she was in the sixth grade. A boy whom she liked said to her, "You're ugly." At Barb's very impressionable age, those words penetrated to her heart. From that moment on she saw herself as less than pretty. She had subconsciously carried that deep hurt with her all these years. Barb knew that the Holy Spirit had now brought the memory to her mind. She instantly understood why she felt the way she did. In that moment God healed Barb from that deep personal wound, and Barb never again saw herself as "ugly."

Some of us have covered hurts or broken areas of our lives so well that they seem normal to us. Perhaps, we are like Barb and have some wounds from what someone has said to us or about us. We may have lived with that judgment rather than living with what our loving Father says about us.

Or, perhaps our early aspirations may have been crushed. Maybe we had failures in our past that we still allow to control how much we are willing to step out and do. All these things and many more can distort our impressions of ourselves. It is hard for us to see ourselves as beautiful creations, designed wonderfully by God our Father.

Some of us aspiring Joshuas and Calebs may still have

lower self-esteem, as Barb did, just when God is calling us to take our positions as spiritual fathers or mothers. To live life fully in the most powerful years of life that God is calling us to, we may need to clear out some of the baggage.

In Mark 4 Jesus shared the parable of the sower and explained how the "cares of this world" stopped believers from having a harvest of thirty-, sixty-, or even a hundred-fold. Any of us in our 50s or 60s or beyond can relate to the cares of this world, which try to interfere with our faith in God's wonderful provision and purposes. These cares, anxieties, hurts, false impressions, etc., stay with us until we cast them off.

First Peter 5:6-7 says, "Therefore humble yourselves under the mighty hand of God, that He may exalt you in due time, casting all your care upon Him, for He cares for you." At our age we all have probably been humbled more than once, by others if not by God. Some of what we walked through we will be able to share with grandchildren or others of a future generation in God's great spiritual lineage. We will carry a Godly authority, not of our own making but because we have persevered, humbled ourselves before God, and have made it this far in our heavenly calling. We will protect future generations from having to walk through some bad things. That is part of God's great plan for our mature years.

Think more about the "casting your cares" portion of the verse, which can include our anxieties, our self-image, and any areas of brokenness.

You may want to take some time alone with the Lord to ask the Holy Spirit to reveal any areas of brokenness and how to be healed. At times, you probably already sensed something wasn't working right in your life, but you didn't know how to define it. It may have been easier to rationalize that your surroundings, circumstances, family, or something else was at fault. Actually, this is part of humbling yourself under the mighty hand of God, that He might exalt you in due time, as 1 Peter 5:6 says.

If you sense you are wounded in some way, I challenge you to start again. Have a new beginning. Hope is ahead. Your destiny is calling you. Clear away the baggage and brokenness.

Another way of addressing potential areas of brokenness is to have some frank conversations with another Christian your age or with Christian friends or a small group your age. In reality, you have nothing to lose and everything to gain. As you already know, God has designed the body of Christ to be joined. You are to be in communion and connection with other members.

Find someone you trust who knows you well. Have a purposeful evening discussion together. Tell the other person or small group that you are preparing for God's next big thing in your life. Let them know you are cleaning out the closet of past hopes and hurts so that you only carry the essentials that will get you to your destination. When you establish a clear understanding for your purposeful time together, ask the other person or small group, "What might be holding me back from being all God called me to be?"

You may have to encourage them to be honest with you. Let them know that you will not judge them for their answers. Also, have paper and pen or a computer with you to capture what they say. Don't let their comments only remain in your short-term memory. Don't treat their responses lightly. Even if they are only half right, take the half that's right. If you feel they have uncovered something of significance, pray together for a release from the hurt or broken area. If you don't know whether they uncovered something, still capture their thoughts and later ask the Lord to give you understanding.

It may also be that you have done something in your earlier years that you think disqualifies you for authority and purpose in your mature years. Joseph's brothers probably thought that way, too. Remember when they went to Egypt to buy food? Genesis 42 through 45 tells the gripping story. Joseph, well disguised in his Egyptian garb, supposedly wants to confirm that the brothers are not spies. He tells them that one of them has to stay in Egypt and will not be returned until the youngest brother, whom they told Joseph about, comes to Egypt. The brothers, not knowing that Joseph understands their language, say to each other,

> *"We are truly guilty concerning our brother, for we saw the anguish of his soul when he pleaded with us, and we would not hear; therefore this distress has come upon us." (Gen 42:21)*

For many years each of them had carried the guilt of having sold Joseph into slavery. You would think they would have gotten over it. But they hadn't. Their treatment of their brother continually haunts each of them.

The brothers bring their youngest brother Benjamin back with them when they return to Egypt to again buy food. And, finally Joseph reveals his real identity to them, as Genesis 45:3-8 records:

> *"I am Joseph; does my father still live?" But his brothers could not answer him, for they were dismayed in his presence. And Joseph said to his brothers, "Please come near to me." So they came near. Then he said: "I am Joseph your brother, whom you sold into Egypt. But now, do not therefore be grieved or angry with yourselves because you sold me here; for God sent me before you to preserve life. For these two years the famine has been in the land, and there are still five years in which there will be neither plowing nor harvesting. And God sent me before you to preserve a posterity for you in the earth, and to save your lives by a great deliverance. So now it was not you who*

sent me here, but God; and He has made me a father to Pharaoh, and Lord of all his house, and a ruler throughout all the land of Egypt.

Sometimes we disqualify ourselves more than God would ever do. As with Joseph's brothers, the sin of the past haunts us and keeps us from living fulfilled and happy lives. Even after Joseph says what happened is all in God's provision, his brothers have a hard time trusting Joseph. Joseph's brothers cannot recognize the blessing coming their way. The sin is too much with them. In this instance their great sin actually sets the wheels in motion for the salvation of their family and ultimately for the safety of the whole Hebrew nation.

You may have sinned a great sin and thus believe God's blessing and provision can no longer be yours. But God's love and grace and the blood of the Cross are all bigger than any of your past sins or mistakes.

For you, the blood of Jesus Christ cleanses you from all sin, as 1 John 1:7 says. You are not to die in past guilt. You are to be set free to do spiritual exploits. You are called to be modern-day Joshuas and Calebs. Jesus himself said, "Therefore if the Son makes you free, you shall be free indeed." (Jn 8:36)

If needed, confront the lie that your sin is greater than God's forgiveness. Declare as the apostle Paul did, "Old things have passed away; behold, all things have become new."

RECOGNIZING THE ENEMY

Where, really, do wounds come from? Yes, I know they come from our interactions with people. But why is this? As a 50+er, we can answer the questions pretty easily. "They are the result of Adam and Eve's fall," we can say, and we would be right. "Satan wants to destroy Christians. Wounds come from him," we can say, and we would be right again. "It's a spiritual battle." Yes, we're right.

So we got the answers right. Why then do so many of us Christian 50+ers still have unhealed wounds? Perhaps a broader answer is that we talk about Satan but don't really understand the war he's waging.

Rick Joyner, the head of MorningStar Ministries in Fort Mill, South Carolina, and a widely respected prophetic leader, wrote some books based on a series of prophetic encounters he had. Below is part of the opening chapter of *The Final Quest*, the first book in his series that recounted his visions. It paints a very vivid picture of the reasons for the wounds—

The demonic army was so large that it stretched as far as I could see. It was separated into divisions, with each carrying a different banner. The foremost divisions marched under the banners of Pride, Self-Righteousness, Respectability, Selfish Ambition, Unrighteous Judgment, and Jealousy. There were many more of these evil divisions beyond my scope of vision, but those in the vanguard of this terrible horde from hell seemed to be the most powerful. The leader of this army was the Accuser of the Brethren himself.

The weapons carried by this horde were also named. The swords were named Intimidation; the spears were named Treachery; and the arrows were named Accusation, Gossip, Slander, and Faultfinding. Scouts and smaller companies of demons with such names as Rejection, Bitterness, Impatience, Unforgiveness, and Lust were sent in advance of this army to prepare for the main attack.

These smaller companies and scouts were much fewer in number, but they were no less powerful than some of the larger divisions that followed. They were smaller only for strategic reasons. Just as John the Baptist was given an extraordinary anointing for baptizing the masses to prepare them for the Lord, these smaller demonic companies were given extraordinary evil powers for "baptizing the masses."

A single demon of Bitterness could sow his poison into multitudes of people, even entire races or cultures. A demon of Lust would attach himself to a single performer, movie, or advertisement and send what appeared to be bolts of electric slime that would hit and "desensitize" great masses of people. All of this was to prepare for the great horde of evil which followed.

Although this army was marching specifically against the church, it also was attacking anyone else that it could. I knew it was seeking to preempt a coming move of God, which was destined to sweep great numbers of people into the church.

The primary strategy of this army was to cause division on every possible level of relationship—churches with each other, congregations with their pastors, husbands and wives, children and parents, and even children with each other. The scouts were sent to locate the openings in churches, families, or individuals that such spirits as Rejection, Bitterness, and Lust could exploit and enlarge. Through these openings would pour demonic influences that completely overwhelmed their victims.

On the Backs of Christians

The most shocking part of this vision was that this horde was not riding on horses, but primarily on Christians!...

The Prisoners

Trailing behind these first divisions was a multitude of other Christians who were prisoners of this army. All of these captive Christians were wounded, and they were guarded by smaller demons of Fear. There seemed to be more prisoners than there were demons in the army.

Surprisingly, these prisoners still had their swords and shields, but they did not use them. It was a shock to see that so many could be kept captive by so few of the little demons of Fear. If the Christians had just used their weapons, they could easily have freed themselves and probably done great damage to the entire evil horde. Instead, they marched along submissively[1]

I encourage you to read *The Final Quest* to help you better understand why Christians become wounded and how to receive healing for yourself and others if you sense you are wounded. You will have a greater revelation of 2 Corinthians 10:3-6:

> *For though we walk in the flesh, we do not war according to the flesh. For the weapons of our warfare are not carnal but mighty in God for pulling down strongholds, casting down arguments and every high thing that exalts itself against the knowledge of God, bringing every thought into captivity to the obedience of Christ.*

We, in fact, have been living the vision that Rick Joyner experienced. In our lifetime many Christians have been wounded and grown passive. And while we have

---

1 Excerpts from Rick Joyner, *The Final Quest*, 6th printing (Fort Mill, SC: MorningStar Publications, 1996), 20-25.

experienced some great revivals and evangelists, we have also been witness to great collapses of ministries. Our culture is now considered post-Christian.

What Satan has been doing is not new. James recognized that believers would fall into many types of trials and that their faith would be tested in such a way that they must look to their Source for the answer. He says, "My brethren, count it all joy when you fall into various trials, knowing that the testing of your faith produces patience. But let patience have its perfect work, that you may be perfect and complete, lacking nothing." (James 1:2-5)

So we now recognize our enemy for who he is. He is a deceiver. He, not the church or other Christians, is our enemy. And though he may have wounded us, we have survived. Satan has tried to divide us. He set a religious spirit among believers to counterfeit the church, and many in the church have succumbed to it.

But we say, "No more." We cast him off and declare that we are children of our loving Father. We appropriate the blood of Jesus over our past. Christ, the head of the Church, is over all principalities and powers.

The apostle Paul instructs, "Beware lest anyone cheat you through philosophy and empty deceit, according to the tradition of men, according to the basic principles of the world, and not according to Christ. For in Him dwells all the fullness of the Godhead bodily; and you are complete in Him, who is the head of all principality and power." (Col 2:8-10)

No more will we tolerate Satan's deceiving ways. He will not wound us. We are healed. Now we get to do exploits that make demons tremble. We will bring healing and hope to those around us and to future generations. We are Joshuas and Calebs.

FURTHER STEPS TO REMOVE WOUNDS

If you sense you still carry some wounds, ask the Holy Spirit to help reveal and heal the wound. I address some common areas below where wounds can occur. I'm sure you can find helpful books written on each of the topics I briefly touch on below. The Holy Spirit will also lead you to others who will join with you in the healing process. As a matter of fact, one of the greatest benefits of walking in wholeness is that we feel restored not only to the Father but to brothers and sisters in the Lord. We have a great journey ahead of us, and we will walk in the strength of the Lord together.

If you are walking in wholeness, bring healing to others who may be struggling with one of the areas below.

Who defines you?

Words have power. God spoke the world into existence. The Patriarchs blessed their children, and it came to pass. God even inhabits the praises (words) of His people.

Many or most of us have been wounded by words at some time in our lives. How we handle what was said may be more important than the harmful words themselves. If we let the harmful words define who we are, they have control over our present and future even when we don't realize it.

Negative words or judgments or beliefs spoken to us from someone we love or respect (such as a parent, close friend, spouse, or spiritual leader) can deeply wound us. For example, some Christian women were marginalized in the '80s because they had to be "submissive" and under a man's authority. They still may have difficulty accepting the authority they have as mature mothers (whether married or single) in the Lord.

Ultimately, it becomes a question of who defines who we really are. God our Father sees us as His son or daughter, uniquely equipped from His hand to walk in love toward Him and others and to be equipped to fulfill a beautiful calling.

If you have been wounded by words and recognize it, one of the steps to being healed is to forgive.

Another step is to define who you really are. Let God define you.

Those who are wounded often use words as a self-defense tool. When God heals us of our hurt, we want to be very careful how we speak. We will speak life-giving statements. We will affirm people. We will offer compliments. We will quote the Word often.

Proverbs 18:21 says, "Death and life are in the power of the tongue, and those who love it will eat its fruit." We break free from the religious spirit and speak life and see Kingdom things happen.

Jesus said, "It is the Spirit who gives life; the flesh profits nothing. The words that I speak to you are spirit, and they are life." (Jn 6:63-64) We will speak life also because what we speak indicates what is in our heart.

Confessing our faults

Really now. Are carrying grudges and bitterness, which lead to death, as important as forgiving, which leads to life and peace and freedom? If you have offended anyone, seek forgiveness.

Confessing our faults to one another is part of God's plan for the body of Christ, as James 5:16 states. God uses interdependency as a way of illustrating the power of union that He wants to have with us.

Wounded people wound people

We have all seen wounded Christians. Perhaps you felt uneasy around them at times, knowing that they make take their hurts out on you or that they have low self-esteem and thus can't relate well to others. One way of recognizing that you have a wound you haven't had the Holy Spirit heal is to look at how you act. Your actions may reveal symptoms of an unhealed wound. I have encountered women who have been abused or mistreated and will no longer trust men. I have seen people criticize almost any Christian activity or Christian endeavor because they were unknowingly releasing anger that was still driven by their unhealed wounds from something suffered at the hands of other Christians.

Second Corinthians 13:5 says, "Examine yourselves as to whether you are in the faith. Test yourselves. Do you not know yourselves, that Jesus Christ is in you?" Do you have a pattern of losing your temper or of constantly criticizing or of feeling you are a "nobody"? What is driving that? Ask the Holy Spirit to reveal the area of brokenness. Then pray that the blood of Jesus Christ, God's Son, will cleanse you from that sin (which may have been done to you). Ask forgiveness for not accepting God's Love to cover that multitude of sins that James 5:19 mentions. Declare freedom from that "woundedness." Mark it on your calendar. And then observe in the days ahead how differently you act and how much more at peace you are.

One way of assuring that other wounds won't develop is to recognize that wounded people wound people. If someone says something false about you, criticizes you, or falsely judges you, consider the source. What wound in them does the Holy Spirit want to heal? Become an angel of hope to them instead of being wounded yourself.

The healing process

The Lord can bring instant healing to you, breaking the power of sin or violation against you that the enemy of your soul has used to hold you back from the fullness of God flowing through you.

There are also times when you must develop a new pattern of behavior, permanently healing the wound in your life and canceling its sting. In these instances you may want to have someone in the body of Christ walk with you as you grow back to health.

Our Father wants all our brokenness or mourning or blindness or captivity or oppression to be healed. The sins, errors, and hurts of the past are to be healed.

And what are some of these areas where we have struggled in the past? Well, I could probably fill a few pages. I'll mention a few of them:

» Divorce or hurt in love relationships
» Parental abuse or other abuse
» Illness
» Loved ones dying
» Children straying
» Being misjudged/broken communications
» Feeling unfulfilled/unclear calling
» Captive to negative thinking
» Addictions
» Lack of finances/lack of security
» Depression/loneliness/orphan spirit

If we have an emotional reaction to one or more items from the above list, it is a sign the wound may still be open. Recognize it. Then get support from someone else in the body of Christ. Satan would love to keep us separated, making us feel sorry for ourselves or thinking we are alone. He wants us to keep things hidden so that he can condemn us. But we can expose his lies and get healing by joining with other children of the Heavenly Father. Darkness flees when the Light enters the circumstance.

You are in control

Do you control the wound, or does it control you? You may have been wounded for so long or so deeply that you feel the wound is part of who you are. It controls your relationship with people, how you act, how you think, how you perceive things. But that's a lie of the enemy. God wants you to prosper and be in health, as 3 John 2 says.

Accept as your truth what the Bible says about you that you can do all things through Christ, as Paul describes in Philippians 4:13. Don't let the wound have power over you by agreeing with it. Cast it off. Declare that the blood of Jesus Christ cleanses us from all sin, as 1 John 1:7 states. This includes the sins committed against us!

The tyranny of the ideal

Only Jesus is perfect. We are in the process. Satan wants us to dwell on our imperfections, making us think we are not worthy. When we strive for the ideal (even an ideal church), we have to be careful that we don't lose hope because we can't achieve it. Focus on the Lord instead of being perfect. You have already seen God's faithfulness in your life in the past, perhaps in some major way such as a healing or an obvious answer to prayer. Dwell on God's love. Anything that God has done for you is much more than what any non-Christian has received. What seems a minor thing to you can be something that will be life changing for a non-Christian. You already have what you need. You don't need to try to perfect yourself before you can walk in authority as a Christian.

You are in a battle

You can't win if you don't have the right weapons. Second Corinthians 10:4-6 says, "For the weapons of our warfare are not carnal but mighty in God for pulling down strongholds, casting down arguments and every high thing that exalts itself against the knowledge of God, bringing every thought into captivity to the obedience of Christ." Learn more about spiritual warfare and the tactics of the enemy. I encourage you to read *The Final Quest*² by Rick Joyner. Written as a series of "prophetic experiences" that Rick had, *The Final Quest* will bring you into a larger and fuller understanding about God's plans and Satan's plans and how we can be aligned with what God is doing.

2 Rick Joyner, *The Final Quest* (Fort Mill, SC: MorningStar Publications, 1996).

HOW DO WE "LOOK" AT OUR AGE?

(I pray that) the Father of glory, may give to you the spirit of wisdom and revelation in the knowledge of Him, the eyes of your understanding being enlightened; that you may know what is the hope of His calling, what are the riches of the glory of His inheritance in the saints, and what is the exceeding greatness of His power toward us who believe, according to the working of His mighty power…(Eph 1:17-19)

How do you think your Heavenly Father sees you? How does a Father who loves his daughter or son so much see that child?

He sees all the potential. I think He smiles a lot when His child (of any age) does something interesting or tries new things or discovers more of who she or he is. Our Heavenly Father, who created us and loves us, wants us to be fulfilled at all stages of life.

Those who look through the lens of religion never see the loving beauty and care of their Heavenly Father. Religion creates a great lens distortion. Love is equated with work and service. Performance rather than relationship becomes most important. We try to prove our love for the Father rather than blessing Him with our love.

It's a question of whether we perceive and judge spiritually or religiously. Probably all of us have encountered people who use religious phrases or conduct or rules to rationalize or explain everything. They then do not have to face personal issues that would force them to change. Religion is a false god. It keeps us from following the first and greatest commandment of loving the LORD our God with all our heart, soul, and mind, as Jesus told the lawyer who had asked Him to identify the greatest commandment. (Matt 22:37)

Every Christian has had to battle religion, that subtle serpent that slithers into our motives and desires, making us believe that we have the answers and can be the determiners of how we love God and each other. Some people read the Bible to apply biblical rules to others rather than to discover more of God for themselves.

The religious lens is removed by having a love relationship with God, as Jesus told the lawyer.

The older, i.e., more mature, I become, the more cautious I am about laying a religious platitude on someone who has an issue. Religion keeps people in bondage or worse. "There is a way that seems right to a man, but its end is the way of death." (Prov 14:12) Religion sounds so good--it must be right; look at the number of people following it. They can use it to give quick answers. They can use it to subjugate others. They can write laws and rules and deal with everything.

Part of being a Joshua or a Caleb is the act of casting off religion. They kept their eyes on God. They believed Him. When everyone else was acting very religiously, they acted righteously. God honored their righteousness and kept them strong through all the years that their religious friends were literally dying off.

We are not under the law but are created new, spiritually new, with new eyes. Just imagine for a moment what it would mean if you personally could help ten people you know remove the religion from their lives and instead walk spiritually, in a deep love relationship with God. Why, you would have some of the greatest fellowship together. You would join with them in prayers and unity and see others' lives changed. Well, when you are radical in your love for God and ruthless with the false god of religion, that can happen. It is part of your calling as the generation who blesses those around them.

We need the Holy Spirit, not religion, to guide us in all truth. As you know, Jesus told his disciples, "When He, the Spirit of truth, has come, He will guide you into all truth; for He will not speak on His own authority, but whatever He hears He will speak; and He will tell you things to come." (Jn 16:13-14) The Holy Spirit will even give you prophetic words for those ten religious people in your life whom God will use you to change. When you compassionately speak the loving truth of God's purposes into their lives, religion can't overcome it.

Religion is a lens distortion.

Another lens distortion is what I call "perception," that is, how we perceive things. A major theme in many of Shakespeare's plays is appearance versus reality. For example, Shakespeare would have a major character dress as someone else, creating a false reality for the other characters. The audience loved the confusion and misunderstanding and even the irony that resulted from one of the characters pretending to be someone else.

For Christians, as well as non-Christians, the perception of how something is can result in acting on the perception as though it is reality. However, unlike non-Christians, Christians have the Holy Spirit to lead them into all truth. Christians alone have access to reality. We are to look beyond outward appearances and actions to instead see the inward man, the man God is calling to come forth.

The apostle Paul addressed the issue of false judgment several times in his letters. In Romans 14 he describes how Christians are judging their brothers and sisters by the food they eat or by the day of the week they choose to set aside for worship. He admonishes them to stop judging others like this and turns the tables by saying to instead be careful that they themselves do not put a stumbling block in someone else's way.

Humans form opinions of others very quickly, often in less than a second. If we don't use a spiritual lens to see others, those quick impressions or perceptions may give us a false understanding of who that person really is or what that person needs. The perception may become the reality distortion that keeps us from ever getting close to that person or really understanding that person. We might see something about that person that doesn't seem right, and we can form a judgment about him or his circumstances or even his spirituality.

Religious people are especially good at forming judgments based on perception. When I was a boy, the religious denomination to which I belonged judged other denominations. Those denominations did not walk in truth the way we did. They did some things that we considered sinful. One of my aunts was in one of those denominations. I never could understand how such a nice person would allow herself to go to that church. Of course, later in life I realized that I had an inaccurate perception of that church.

Another great lens distortion is bias. While perceptions can be formed very quickly, biases take longer. At our age we have established many very deeply rooted impressions. They may be associated with a location we've lived for many years, they may be tied to a type of church we've attended, they may be part of a racial or ethnic group, they may be related to our vocation or income level, and so forth. These deep impressions can create a type of bias if we are not actively aware of them. To walk in our calling as our Father has intended, our eyes have to be free of personal prejudices, biases, and discrimination. That does not mean we have to relate to everyone and be everyone's close friend. But it does mean that we see every member of the body of Christ as special. We also realize every human being is created in the image of God and that He loves them.

When I was growing up, we made fun of the ethnic origin of most of the people in a town just 30 minutes from our town. We also told jokes about people from other states. These juvenile attitudes are easy to understand and overcome. However, it may be much more difficult to see beyond a frame of reference that has been established over decades.

In our 43 years of marriage Barb and I lived in nine different states. We connected with many different ethnic, racial, and cultural groups, not to mention the different types of churches we attended. I witnessed racial and sexual discrimination and heard many racial or ethnic slurs. I saw how Barb felt marginalized in a Southern culture where men often treated women dismissively.

At every age, and at our age especially, we need the Holy Spirit to give us eyes of compassion for everyone we see. Biases separate people from each other. A bias is a way of making yourself superior to someone else by belittling the other person. That is wrong and that is sin.

Proverbs 16:2 says, "All the ways of a man are pure in his own eyes, but the LORD weighs the spirits." Our biases make us look good to ourselves. Others may not measure up to our standards. We need the Holy Spirit as the arbiter of what is right. We can judge in the Spirit or from a framework of personal prejudice. At our age we choose the Spirit.

Victims of prejudice, discrimination, or bias also have to make decisions about how they respond. To walk in the destiny God has for us right now, we have to be healed from bitterness against a person or group who has harmed us. Many of us have experienced discrimination because we were a certain race or sex or age; we were not married, we were divorced; we came from the "outside" into the community; we had more (or less) money than those around us; we had more (or less) education than others.

It can be hard to forgive those who have falsely accused or judged us, whether it is one individual or a whole class of society. They have hurt us and perhaps limited our success or opportunities. But God calls us to forgive, just as Jesus forgave.

If you recognize you are acting partially through the lens of bias or if you have been a victim of bias and haven't forgiven as you should, the Father is ready to forgive. The blood of Jesus Christ, His Son, cleanses us from all sin. Simply ask forgiveness, appropriating that blood to your circumstance.

There are some ways of recognizing when we have been forgiven and changed. Racial or ethnic or sexual or cultural humor won't be as funny anymore. But one of the greatest indicators is compassion. Just as Jesus had compassion for us, you will find that a new compassion develops in you, even for those types of individuals or groups who have hurt you. This is not natural. It is spiritual. And that's who we are. We are spiritual, operating from the realm of the Spirit instead of from the flesh. As a result, we get to change attitudes around us. We get to bring healing to those who were discriminated against. We get to operate in the authority of the Spirit. And that's what we want to do in the second half-century of our lives!

Many, if not most, of us in our second half century have lost some eyesight. Our vision becomes weaker, and we need glasses or some other means to help correct our vision.

God wants to help us with that. He desires "vision" to be restored. He wants to give us greater vision and understanding for who we are and how He has equipped us. He wants us to see ourselves as He sees us. Each one of us is His special child, now grown up in Him. We are equipped for Kingdom authority and power, developed through love. The mantle of authority He is giving us fits. We can see that clearly when our spiritual lenses are not clouded or broken.

LOOKING FORWARD

At our mature age it might seem easier to look back than to look forward. After all, so much has happened, and we do not know what lies ahead. It could be more comforting and comfortable to reminisce instead of think about a future that shortens every day.

But God's plans for what we get to do are going to happen in the days ahead.

Which direction do you look? Can you anticipate that God has something for you ahead?

I have normally been a future-oriented person. I have always liked new things. It was not extremely hard to live all over the nation and own, and many times fix up, 15 different homes. When people ask me what my favorite place to live was, I normally respond that wherever I'm living is a good place. There are special memories and attraction to each place from the past, but I do not live in the past. I live in the present and anticipate the future.

As I write this, the present is very important to me. I am living in a season where God's mercies are new every morning.

In 2011 Barbara, my bride of 43 years, went to heaven after a tough battle with cancer. I had to work through the grief and emotions. For me every day had to be a new day. On the mirror in my bathroom I have a declaration that I still recite every morning as I prepare for the day. It is:

I am part of the ecclesia, the governing body of the Lord. I govern in the Kingdom under the Father's authority.

Father, I am ready for today's marching orders and will bring the Kingdom.

I contend for the miracles I read in the Word.

I call forth words of knowledge. I call forth healing.

My eyes are holy unto the Lord. I see spiritually.

I carry the atmosphere of the Lord and see many lives changed.

I declare nations coming into the Kingdom.

For those who have suffered loss or been hurt, it can be easy to live in the past, reminiscing about better days, days we remember fondly, even if we are no longer accurate about how some of those times were actually spent. At our age, however, we still have to make daily choices that determine our happiness and purpose.

We can choose to look forward instead of backward. Yes, there are beautiful memories we can cherish. But our future does not have to be determined by our past. Otherwise, the verse that "old things have passed away; behold, all things are become new" would not be truth. We cannot change the past. Living there constantly won't do one thing to change its outcome. Instead, we make the same choice Paul made: One thing I do, forgetting those things which are behind and reaching forward to those things which are ahead, I press toward the goal for the prize of the upward call of God in Christ Jesus. (Phil 3:13-14)

Of course that does not mean I don't cherish my beautiful wife's memory and love. She and I were one. But it does mean I don't camp in the past. Each one of us is to be reaching for something greater in the future that our Father has placed there for us. Our eyes are to be fixed on the Kingdom. We live to obtain the prize.

When looking forward rather than backward, we see things differently than the world sees them. We anticipate God's plan being fulfilled in us.

We declare blessings to future generations. We act as elders in the gates, providing life-giving words of wisdom. We tell stories to future generations of God's faithfulness. And so much more we get to do.

I was recently with a Christian who had anxiety about what the future held. She has a married daughter who calls her often and shares some of the day's emergencies and problems. This Christian mother develops instant anxiety. I have heard her verbalize what the possible outcome of the given circumstances might be. She mentally creates a negative future outcome and then almost panics at the possibility. She has a way of believing that things will turn out wrong. Of course, most of what she conjures up will never happen, but somehow this mother can't help but develop these false scenarios.

Perhaps it's that she wants to be the one who will solve the problem and save her daughter. Maybe she wants to show her daughter that she is there for her. Whatever the reason, this mother lives in nearly constant anxiety and worry.

It's often not hard to be anxious about the future. At our age we can worry that we won't have any retirement, that we will have major medical issues, that our children will turn out wrong, that the economy will crash and we'll be destitute, that we won't be useful anymore, that _____ (you fill in the blank).

The New International Version of the Bible translates the word *care* differently in 1 Peter 5:7. It says, "Cast all your **anxiety** on him because he cares for you." For many of us this verse is a daily reminder of the action we must take.

As Christians we know bad things happen. We know there is evil in the world and an adversary who goes about as a roaring lion seeking whom he might devour.

We, however, choose to obey our Lord's direction:

But seek first the kingdom of God and His righteousness, and all these things shall be added to you. Therefore do not worry about tomorrow, for tomorrow will worry about its own things. Sufficient for the day is its own trouble. (Matt 6:33-34)

With all of life's possible issues, we will choose to place our minds under the Spirit's control, "Casting down imaginations, and every high thing that exalteth itself against the knowledge of God, and bringing into captivity every thought to the obedience of Christ." (2 Cor 10:5, KJV)

More than 30 years ago Barb and I were going through a very, very difficult time in our spiritual lives. We were confused about our circumstances and wondered what the future held. During this crucial time, the Lord illuminated Psalm 32:8 to me, and it has become one of my life verses:

I will instruct you and teach you in the way you should go;
I will guide you with My eye.

Truly, the LORD is our Shepherd. He will lead us in the days ahead, no matter what the circumstance. We are going to take spiritual ground in the future. We anticipate good things from His hands. We even lead others into God's promised land for them.

LOOKING OUTWARD

As we move through life, we may start living more defensively. It's like we want to build a bubble of safety about ourselves because it is so difficult to handle all of life. At times that defensive posture means we no longer step out to make new friends, learn new things, or take chances

For Christians, the scene may look like this: you are always with other Christians, your communication is with other Christians, all your experiences are with other Christians. Another way of saying it is that you live your life inside the church walls. It is easier to live within the camp than to be a scout. (It's also called being in a rut.)

Stepping into different surroundings or circumstances keeps us growing and moving and challenged. Not only is our mind more active as we live outward; our spirit is as well. We get to see more things through spiritual eyes. We get to do the work rather than reminiscing about how work used to be done. In other words, we live. We also continue to have greater perspective about what our Heavenly Father is up to, as well as increased perspective about ourselves.

Living outward may mean going on a short missions trip to help some orphans or abused women. It may mean being available to talk with younger business people. It may mean praying for our server at the table in the restaurant. It will mean something different for each person. It doesn't have to be some "great" adventure. It simply means to continue to reach out.

Living outside our bubble of safety may also expose some of the issues we ignored or didn't see because we were so used to our circumstances. Barbara and I moved to South Carolina in 2009 to be part of MorningStar Ministries, in Fort Mill. I quickly recognized that although Barbara and I knew we were called there, we still had areas in our lives God wanted to address and heal. MorningStar is a wonderful place for spiritual healing and growth to occur because of the non-judgmental atmosphere. As we stepped into more of what God wanted, we were changed for the better.

Because Barbara and I lived in nine different states over the years, we had to take the initiative to make friends. Most people were already living their established patterns and didn't necessarily look to change things. So, when we went to a new church, we became our own "greeters." Wherever we sat, we actively engaged in conversations with others around us. Usually a friendship opening occurred, and we got to go to lunch with someone we just met or have them over to our house. We had realized very early in our married lives that most people weren't going to reach out to us. We needed to take the initiative.

There were exceptions, however, which surprised us and made us feel God's special love for us. When we first moved to the Chicago area, we started attending a church in the area near Lake Michigan where we wanted to relocate. But we first had to sell our other home in Indiana. Consequently, we were renting an apartment about an hour from where we wanted to live on the North Shore, which also meant an hour from the church. The first or second Sunday we attended the church, we met a couple and had a nice conversation.

The next Saturday the husband showed up at our distant suburban apartment. He said he "just happened" to be in the neighborhood and had with him some special pancake mix and all the fixings and wondered if we could use them for a healthy weekend breakfast. Barb and I were both surprised and honored by what this man had done. We had only had a short conversation at church. This man and his wife were living their lives outside the church walls. They reached out to people rather than sitting back waiting to be reached. I've now known this man for more than 15 years. He continues to reach out to people. He and his wife are both vibrant, no doubt because they are looking outward and seeing what God would have them do each day.

He recently told me that one of his "life" verses is Lamentations 3:23, "(God's mercies) are new every morning." All things become new to him every day. He anticipates that God is going to do something through him. I have watched him mentor those younger than he and reach out to many other people. He shows God's mercies wherever he goes.

We get to do the same. Sometimes it is just a kind look. It may be a non-judgmental attitude when you meet someone. It could be a smile, demonstrating we are pleased to be in their company. It could be a prophetic word that we speak into their lives. Whatever it is, the point is that we are looking outward instead of inward. We see and love the body of Christ, and we see and love those who are yet to be reconciled to the Father.

We have a choice every morning. We can live in introspection, saddened at our physical, mental, or emotional condition. We can live the safe life, protecting ourselves from the world or potential harm. On the other hand, we can declare God's mercies new every morning and can carry His mercy and love wherever we are, looking outward, anticipating the next encounter we are going to have with someone else, recognizing that we are carrying the Answer.

A great way to start each day looking outward is to write a declaration and post it where you can read it. It can be a verse the Holy Spirit has illuminated to you. It can be a series of God-centered affirmations. It will be unique to you. Make certain it is a declaration that aligns with your position as a son or daughter of the Father. A person can declare health and happiness and not be a Christian. What does the Father want you to declare? What verses of Scripture has the Holy Spirit quickened to you that will lead you to health and fulfillment? What is there that leads you into the fullness of who you are as a son or daughter of the Father, as an heir of salvation in the Kingdom? Write these down and post them. Declare them each morning to establish your day.

Declare you are part of the Joshua and Caleb generation.

Section II:

Applying God's Purposes

FULLY EQUIPPED

Therefore take up the whole armor of God, that you may be able to withstand in the evil day, and having done all, to stand.(Eph 6:13)

When I was young, I sometimes watched parents disciplining (or not disciplining) their children. "I'd never let my child do that," I muttered more than once. Later, as a father of a very active boy, I discovered that now I was the one being muttered about.

It would be great if we all had good role models who showed us how to be good parents or understanding and mature adults. But, alas, that's not always the case. For each stage of life, it would be great to have examples of how to live. Now that we have entered the second half-century of our lives, who do we look to for guidance? If you are like me, you start remembering your grandparents or someone else who has now gone to heaven, remembering some of the encouraging words they had or that special sweetness that they carried. You may even wonder at times if you can live your life to the end as graciously as they did.

The answer is that you can and will, and you will walk in power and authority, love and compassion, wisdom and understanding, gentleness and strength, and mercy and grace the rest of your life. That will happen because that is what God has been preparing you for throughout your life.

What if your whole life has been a preparation for doing some remarkable things in your senior years? The Bible records two such examples when Joseph and Mary present the baby Jesus in the Temple. The second chapter of Luke records the story:

> *And behold, there was a man in Jerusalem whose name was Simeon, and this man was just and devout, waiting for the Consolation of Israel, and the Holy Spirit was upon him. And it had been revealed to him by the Holy Spirit that he would not see death before he had seen the* LORD's *Christ. So he came by the Spirit into the temple. And when the parents brought in the Child Jesus, to do for Him according to the custom of the law, he took Him up in his arms and blessed God and said:*

> *"*LORD, *now You are letting Your servant depart in peace, according to Your word; for my eyes have seen Your salvation which You have prepared before the face of all peoples, a light to bring revelation to the Gentiles, and the glory of Your people Israel."*

> *And Joseph and His mother marveled at those things which were spoken of Him. Then Simeon blessed them, and said to Mary His mother, "Behold, this Child is destined for the fall and rising of many in Israel, and for a sign which will be spoken against (yes, a sword will pierce through your own soul also), that the thoughts of many hearts may be revealed." (Luke 2: 25-35)*

Just think. All his life Simeon had watched the Jewish nation put on a religious spectacle. This was cultural religion on a grand scale. There was a lot of show and many rules but no love and power. He must have grieved when those around him did not carry the same passion for God that he did. When the Temple was desecrated with such things as moneychangers, he probably carried the burden even more deeply. But what could he do? He was only one man. He did not want to desert his fellow Jews. After all, they together were God's chosen people, weren't they?

Simeon reminds me of some Christians who are firmly in the second half of their lives. They've always wanted the church to be vibrant and full of love and power. When their leaders sometimes did things that seemed to have the wrong motives or worse, they prayed for the leadership and kept on looking to God instead of to men. They, like Simeon, lived a just life and walked in devotion to God.

And, like Simeon, they will get to do some remarkable things. He held the baby Jesus. Simeon held the vulnerable baby Jesus. God allowed this just, old man to hold the Savior of the World. The Holy Spirit was on Simeon, and God had prophesied to Simeon that before he died, he was going to see Christ.

What if God has that for you to do, too? What if He allows you to lift up the fragile baby Jesus in one of your grandchildren's lives or in the life of another younger person or new convert? What if He allows you to bless the parents as Simeon did? Will you be ready? Yes, you will be. All things are leading to this time in your life. You are going to get to do things you never could have done if you were younger!

The second example is Anna. Luke 2:36-38 continues the story:

Now there was one, Anna, a prophetess, the daughter of Phanuel, of the tribe of Asher. She was of a great age, and had lived with a husband seven years from her virginity; and this woman was a widow of about eighty-four years, who did not depart from the temple, but served God with fastings and prayers night and day. And coming in that instant she gave thanks to the LORD, *and spoke of Him to all those who looked for redemption in Jerusalem.*

Anna had gone through a lot in her life, including losing the husband she loved. But she didn't lose her love for God. She served Him faithfully, despite the distorted religious circumstances surrounding her at the time. When she saw the baby Jesus, her heart must have skipped a beat as she immediately recognized the Savior of the world. Instantly she gave thanks to the LORD. And then she prophesied, telling every person willing to hear who this baby Jesus was.

So, how did she learn to prophesy so powerfully that even canon Scripture records it? Had she attended prophecy school? I'm guessing she hadn't. She was close to God. She could recognize His voice and His impulse moving through her.

It's the same for us today. As we continue to stay close to the Lord, loving Him in all our circumstances, He directs us. He may give us a word for someone. He may inspire us with a corporate word for a small group. He may use us to give direction to our grandchildren. We "walk in the Spirit," as Galatians 5:16-26 so beautifully describes, blessing others by sharing the fruit of our closeness with Him.

A friend of mine told me how he had finally identified God's hand in his life. He is about 58 and has been a Christian for many years. He told me that it wasn't until about 8 years ago that he realized he had been hearing the Spirit's voice for years. He just did not know how to recognize it. Looking back, he could think of decisions he made that he now realizes were made because the Holy Spirit was leading him.

I'm thinking Anna, the prophetess, also became a better spokesperson for God the closer and longer her relationship developed with Him.

We get to tell other generations how God worked in

our lives and is continuing to work in us. We get to speak prophetically into others' lives. Anna didn't have to think, "Is God telling me that this baby is His Son? I wonder if I should say something?" She was so close to God that words came from her as soon as she saw the baby.

We continually grow in our understanding of God's hand in our lives and how He speaks to us. I know He delights in revealing more of himself to us as we mature and are able to comprehend what He is saying.

This past year I went on a marvelous fly-fishing vacation with my son and some friends. One of the days we drifted the legendary Blackfoot River in Montana, floating through the same waters that are described in the book, *A River Runs Through It*.

At the end of the float, I got out of the drift boat and gathered up my belongings. I grabbed my long-sleeved Orvis fishing shirt that I had taken off early in the heat of the day. I had this slight impression sweep through my mind to check my glasses. It was so slight that I ignored it and kept packing. Later I looked for my glasses and realized they must have fallen out by the river's edge when I took off my shirt.

The next day I was fly-fishing again. I had just put on a new fly and dipped it in a liquid that would keep it waterproof so that it stayed on the surface. I did some false casts, waving the fly through the air on the end of the line to dry it off and permanently waterproof it to make it float better before I used it. The same kind of fleeting impression swept through my mind, warning me that I would snag the fly on a limb across the narrow stream I was fishing. I ignored the impression, and about five seconds later I snagged the fly on the limb and lost it.

Then I realized the Holy Spirit had, in a very, very subtle way, been trying to help me on both occasions. I was not used to recognizing the Spirit's whisper-like impressions that way (especially while fishing) and learned the hard way. I know many of you can tell stories of how you learned to hear or recognize God's voice when He spoke to you. When I was younger, I didn't know all these things. I grew up in a Pentecostal church that had prescribed or cultural times for letting the Holy Spirit speak a prophetic word through a person. But as we seek the Lord and stay close to His heart, we learn new things from Him and develop more intimacy.

The Teacher continues to teach us and lead us into all Truth. We get to walk in the truth and to help others. Our 50+ group at MorningStar Ministries prayed for each graduating senior in the high school and at MorningStar University. As we spoke and prayed individual blessings over them, I could hear prophetic words coming from the 50+ers. They weren't trying to be prophetic. They were prophetic. And they also operated with discernment as they blessed the younger generation.

In Ephesians 4 the apostle Paul explains what the spiritual journey of the Joshua and Caleb generation should look like. He recognizes that we will mature, and, as verse 13 describes, "come to the unity of the faith and of the knowledge of the Son of God, to a perfect man, to the measure of the stature of the fullness of Christ."

We will "no longer be children, tossed to and fro and carried about with every wind of doctrine, by the trickery of men, in the cunning craftiness of deceitful plotting, but, speaking the truth in love, may grow up in all things into Him who is the head — Christ — from whom the whole body, joined and knit together by what every joint supplies, according to the effective working by which every part does its share, causes growth of the body for the edifying of itself in love." (Eph 4:14-16)

We, at our mature age, continue growing up "in all things." We're no longer tossed about by various doctrines. We are at a point in our maturity that we can measure ourselves against "the stature of the fullness of Christ," not measuring as others might measure but as our loving Heavenly Father would measure, with His tape measure of love that recognizes all you have gone through.

So we, "speaking the truth in love," continue to grow in all things into Christ, "who is the head." Verse 16 of Ephesians 4 explains that each part of the body of Christ supplies something and causes growth to the body. So, here's the rub. We don't have a choice. We are called to stand in our position at our age so that the body of Christ grows through love.

Not only are we somebody. We are absolutely necessary. His mantle of authority is on our lives.

HEALED TO BE A BLESSING

Luke 4:16-22 contains a powerful interaction between Jesus and his hometown people. The incident and Jesus' words have a direct application of who we are now to be. Here's the story:

So He came to Nazareth, where He had been brought up. And as His custom was, He went into the synagogue on the Sabbath day, and stood up to read. And He was handed the book of the prophet Isaiah. And when He had opened the book, He found the place where it was written:

"The Spirit of the LORD is upon Me, because He has anointed Me to preach the gospel to the poor; He has sent Me to heal the brokenhearted, to proclaim liberty to the captives and recovery of sight to the blind, to set at liberty those who are oppressed; to proclaim the acceptable year of the LORD."

Then He closed the book, and gave it back to the attendant and sat down. And the eyes of all who were in the synagogue were fixed on Him. And He began to say to them, "Today this Scripture is fulfilled in your hearing."

Jesus returns to his hometown, the town where he grew up. But he is different now. Much has happened in his life just as much has happened in our lives. He steps from His past and how people remembered Him and proclaims who He is now. He is the anointed One who announces the good news of the Kingdom to us. He heals the brokenhearted and proclaims liberty to the oppressed. He restores our sight and sets us free.

His actions and words are a fulfillment Isaiah's prophetic pronouncement. Jesus is actually quoting Isaiah 61, which says:

The Spirit of the LORD God is upon Me, because the LORD has anointed Me to preach good tidings to the poor; He has sent Me to heal the brokenhearted, to proclaim liberty to the captives, and the opening of the prison to those who are bound; to proclaim the acceptable year of the LORD, and the day of vengeance of our God; to comfort all who mourn, to console those who mourn in Zion, to give them beauty for ashes, the oil of joy for mourning, the garment of praise for the spirit of heaviness. (Isaiah 61:1-3)

Just as the word from Isaiah 61 prophesied who the coming Jesus was to be, Jesus' words in Luke 4 are a prophetic word for us, prophesying who we now are to be. Jesus modeled how to change from the past to now walking in our calling when He read the Scripture to his hometown. The prophetic words that He spoke to them are a call for us to also walk in our calling as the Joshua and Caleb generation, leaving things of the past.

Jesus could have let the townspeople run his life. He could have let situations from the past dictate or limit his future. He could have come back to Nazareth to settle down.

Hey, he had done some traveling, but now it's time to get to work and be a good master carpenter. But He knew there was a great calling on His life. Things of the past were not going to deter Him from His future.

He wants the same to apply to us. Many in Nazareth probably wanted Jesus to be how they remembered him. They did not understand how He had changed into the Man He now was.

We also have voices reminding us of our past. They let us know we're not perfect, that we have failed, that we have hurt others, that we should not be so different. The accuser of the brethren is the voice of condemnation. He will speak to us as long as we will listen. He wants to keep us wounded and dwelling on our failures. He attempts to drown out Jesus' words to us that He has been anointed to set us free.

But we will not believe Satan's lies. We will turn off his invasive thoughts as soon as they enter our minds. Instead, we will hear Jesus saying that He came to set us free, that His blood covers a multitude of sins, that we are being conformed to His likeness.

Isaiah 61:3 tells the result of accepting Jesus' healing words and stepping into our purpose just as He stepped into His purpose: "that they may be called trees of righteousness, the planting of the LORD, that He may be glorified."

We are to be trees of righteousness. We are the planting of the LORD. We are not saplings. We are not some new growth. No, our age and experience in the LORD, our battles in life, our hurts and frustrations, have all contributed to making us mature. We are trees — trees of righteousness. He has planted us. And now as Joshuas and Calebs we get to return glory to Him.

Once Jesus has touched and restored us, we get to pass it on. We are now the ones to heal broken hearts, set others free, restore their sight, break oppression from their lives, and much more.

Isaiah 61 continues to describe more of what these healed and set-at-liberty people get to do—what we get to do:

And they shall rebuild the old ruins, they shall raise up the former desolations, and they shall repair the ruined cities, the desolations of many generations. (Isaiah 61:4)

Really, the old things are passed away, and all things are becoming new. What was ruined will be recreated, rebuilt, and restored the way it should be. The "former desolations"-- those broken relationships and dead areas from the past—will be transformed. We will even tackle things beyond our family and friends, repairing the lives of entire cities.

We, as the Joshua and Caleb generation, also get to set the standard for future generations. The "desolations of many generations" are passed away. All things in future generations "are become new" because of who we are.

We, like our Savior, stand between the old and the new, ending the deadness and hurts of the past and releasing future generations into their Godly calling. Yes, we, because of our calling in Christ, get to do these things. We won't let anyone marginalize us ever again. We stand in our calling. The Holy Spirit is releasing us into our fullness.

And what's the payoff (if what I've said isn't already enough)? The rest of Isaiah 61 states it. It is worth pinning the entire passage to the bathroom mirror, allowing those promises and declarations to start the day. Here are some parts of it for us, the Joshua and Caleb generation:

Strangers shall stand and feed your flocks, and the sons of the foreigner shall be your plowmen and your vinedressers.

You shall be named the priests of the LORD. They shall call you the servants of our God.

*Instead of your shame you shall have **double honor**, and instead of confusion they shall rejoice in their portion.*

*In their land they shall **possess double**; everlasting joy shall be theirs.*

"For I, the LORD, I will direct their work in truth, and will make with them an everlasting covenant. Their descendants shall be known among the Gentiles, and their offspring among the people. All who see them shall acknowledge them, that they are the posterity whom the LORD has blessed." (excerpts from Isaiah 61:5-11, emphases mine)

God is making provision for us. Just when some new ache in our body tells us we're aging some, the Spirit says our descendants will be known and blessed.

YOUR CALLING TO BLESS FUTURE GENERATIONS

And He led them out as far as Bethany, and He lifted up His hands and blessed them. Now it came to pass, while He blessed them, that He was parted from them and carried up into heaven (Luke 24:50-52)

I can picture Jesus' final act on earth. He raises hands and blesses those who will remain. He blesses all of us through those watching Him ascend to the Father. He is blessing His bride to be.

A remarkably beautiful part of our calling is to also bless future generations.

Some of us, however, may not perceive the gifting that is in us. Unlike married couples whose status changes to that of parents the instant they hear their baby's first cries, we become spiritual parents over time. And, spiritual parenting is not widely seen or understood in the church at large. Consequently, some of us 50+ers don't recognize the spiritual mantle we are actually wearing, either.

We, however, have walked with the Lord for years. We are not like "children being tossed about with every wind of doctrine" or by other people's crafty speech, as Ephesians 4:14 describes. We are spiritual parents to future generations. Let's just clarify what we look like.

I'll use examples of two spiritual fathers, simply to help define a spiritual parent.

First, there is Father God himself. A spiritual parent will create spiritual children who have a spiritual DNA. Genesis describes the circumstances:

> *Then God said, "Let Us make man in Our image, according to Our likeness; let them have dominion over the fish of the sea, over the birds of the air, and over the cattle, over all the earth and over every creeping thing that creeps on the earth." So God created man in His own image; in the image of God He created him; male and female He created them. Then God blessed them, and God said to them, "Be fruitful and multiply; fill the earth and subdue it; have dominion over the fish of the sea, over the birds of the air, and over every living thing that moves on the earth." (Gen 1:26-28)*

We, like God the Father, want to see spiritual offspring. Our hearts are focused on future generations, knowing the potential they have and the love they will be able to give back. We, like the Father, want them to walk in our image spiritually. We, like the Father, bless them, speaking power, fruitfulness, and multiplication into their futures, ordaining them to their place of dominion as sons and daughters of the Father, living with Kingdom authority.

Jesus described the Father's importance in his own life. He said,

> *The Son can do nothing of Himself, but what He sees the Father do; for whatever He does, the Son also does in like manner. For the Father loves the Son, and shows Him*

*all things that He Himself does; and He will show Him
greater works than these, that you may marvel. (John
5:19-20)*

A spiritual parent is a model for the spiritual child. And
the spiritual parent loves the child.

A spiritual parent also supplies the child with the appropriate good things, as Jesus again describes:

*What man is there among you who, if his son asks for
bread, will give him a stone? Or if he asks for a fish, will
he give him a serpent? If you then, being evil, know how
to give good gifts to your children, how much more will
your Father who is in heaven give good things to those
who ask Him! (Matt 7:9-12)*

God, our spiritual Father, gives good things to His children. We as spiritual parents do the same thing.

A second example of a spiritual parent is the apostle Paul.

He didn't start out that way, however. He tells his spiritual son Timothy, "This is a faithful saying and worthy of
all acceptance, that Christ Jesus came into the world to save
sinners, of whom I am chief." (1 Tim 1:15-16) Many of us
probably started out like Paul. We did things that were
totally contrary to what God would have us do. Paul actually helped murder Christians. Yet, God made him a spiritual father. There is hope for each one of us to walk in the
calling of God as a spiritual parent. Because Christ's sacri-
fice is so powerful, the multitude of sins we had are covered. We discovered that long ago. All things continually
become new in all our circumstances. We get to share all
that with spiritual offspring that they, too, may understand
God's unfailing love.

Let's review some of Paul's acts as a spiritual parent.

The verses I just quoted demonstrated Paul's transpar-
ency. He is writing to his spiritual son in the faith but doesn't

brag. He doesn't have to be the perfect example. He simply has to be himself. He readily admits that he has sinned. As we've all probably discovered by now, people have a great capacity for forgiveness. But if you are a hypocrite or refuse to repent or apologize, people don't trust you. Paul was honest and open.

As a spiritual father, Paul had deep love for those who were younger in the faith. Paul actually used the birth metaphor to describe his deep concerns and love toward spiritual children. To the Galatians he writes, "My little children, of whom I travail in birth again until Christ be formed in you, I desire to be present with you now, and to change my voice; for I stand in doubt of you." (Gal. 4:19-20, KJV) Paul "travailed in birth" for spiritual children, wanting them to grow in God. Our Heavenly Father wants us to have the same deep feelings toward future generations. Their spiritual growth and maturity should be a focal point of our own existence.

Paul also recognized that spiritual children look to and imitate spiritual fathers and mothers, just as Jesus did what he saw the Father doing. Paul says to the Philippian church, "Brethren, join in following my example, and note those who so walk, as you have us for a pattern. For many walk, of whom I have told you often, and now tell you even weeping, that they are the enemies of the cross of Christ." (Phil 3:17-19) Paul's heart was so big. He wept when he saw those who refused to recognize Jesus as the Messiah. He wanted everyone to be born again. He would gladly be a spiritual father to them.

Paul's parental oversight is also demonstrated in one of his letters to the Corinthians.

I do not write these things to shame you, but as my beloved children I warn you. For though you might have ten thousand instructors in Christ, yet you do not have many fathers; for in Christ Jesus I have begotten you through the gospel. Therefore I urge you, imitate me. For this reason I have sent Timothy to you, who is my beloved and faithful son in the LORD, who will remind you of my ways in Christ, as I teach everywhere in every church. (1 Cor 4:14-17)

Paul had fathered many spiritual children. He was more than a Sunday school teacher to them, more than someone who told them how to live. He had birthed them. He was not afraid to have them imitate the things he did. He even sent his special son in the faith, Timothy, to tell them stories of how Paul acted as a spiritual father.

We may not have birthed many spiritual children. We might have ruled ourselves out as spiritual parents. We may think that Paul is special and that we could never compare ourselves to him or do what he did. If we think that way, we are wrong.

Our society and cultural Christianity have fostered a lot of spiritual orphans. They are not connected to spiritual parents, although they want to be. In each person, God the Father has placed a spiritually genetic desire to be connected to spiritual parents. We are the parents they are to be connected to. We can adopt any of them spiritually, becoming a spiritual parent to them. Our lives modeled before them, our stories told in tenderness to them, our acts demonstrated through compassion for them all form bonds of love between spiritual children and us, their spiritual parents.

We have learned so much along the way. Our hearts for them compel us to share the stories of God's faithfulness. It's so much easier than we may think. We simply recognize them, by saying hello, by going out of our way to acknowledge their existence. They respond.

This is part of our calling. It is part of the "all things are becoming new" in our lives. God is placing us here right now for this important assignment. It took years for us to mature in the Lord to our present position. Now, more than at any time in our lives, we get to give away the spiritual truth that the Holy Spirit has shown us.

Some of us may think our time on earth is short--that we can't impact a future generation. Well, the apostle Paul had similar thoughts. He writes the Philippians:

For to me, to live is Christ, and to die is gain. But if I live on in the flesh, this will mean fruit from my labor; yet what I shall choose I cannot tell. For I am hard-pressed between the two, having a desire to depart and be with Christ, which is far better. Nevertheless to remain in the flesh is more needful for you. (Phil 1:21-25)

Paul, who had done so much, could have said, "Take me to heaven, Lord. I'm done here." Instead, he realizes that some spiritual children are still in need of a dad.

Some of us might not consider ourselves as worthy because we most likely have not lived a perfect life. In the '70s, during the height of the charismatic renewal, we talked about the difference between carnal Christians and those who followed the Spirit. Of course, I was always on the side of those who "followed the Spirit." Later in life I looked back and saw that though I desired a walk of "life in the Spirit," I sometimes fell short. I, however, will not live in condemnation.

I stand in what Paul wrote in Romans 8.

There is therefore now no condemnation to those who are in Christ Jesus, who do not walk according to the flesh, but according to the Spirit. For the law of the Spirit of life in Christ Jesus has made me free from the law of sin and death. For what the law could not do in that it was weak through the flesh, God did by sending His own Son in the likeness of sinful flesh, on account of sin: He condemned sin in the flesh, that the righteous requirement of the law might be fulfilled in us who do not walk according to the flesh but according to the Spirit. For those who live according to the flesh set their minds on the things of the flesh, but those who live according to the Spirit, the things of the Spirit. For to be carnally minded is death, but to be spiritually minded is life and peace. (Rom 8:1-6)

Our hearts are after God. The enemy of our soul wants to speak condemnation into our ears and hearts. He asks, "How can you be a true spiritual parent when you failed yourself at times? How can you act as a father or mother in the Lord when one of your children is not 'serving' the Lord?"

So much condemnation can come at us if we let it. I simply declare Romans 8:2 over myself: The law of the Spirit of Life in Christ Jesus has made me free from the law of sin and death.

A dear friend of mine was a missionary for years. She was an eyewitness to many major miracles on the mission field in the very early days of the worldwide sweep of the Spirit that was dubbed the charismatic movement. The missions board of her denomination had told her and her husband they had to leave their children behind in a boarding school and only visit them from time to time because that is what missionaries are called to do.

The couple obeyed the missions board and were separated from their children, except for occasional visits for several years. The missions board of that denomination later recognized the error in separating the parents from the children and rescinded the restriction. The damage had been done, however. Some of this woman's children still carry deep wounds, even after many years.

The past half-century of Christianity in America has not been very pretty at times. We often gave way to the spirit of religion or felt that spirit's heavy oppression. Today we have survived those battles. We will not let Satan condemn us. We've been there, done that. And we won't let Satan do that to our children, either.

We declare freedom from the past and freedom from the serpent. "Therefore if the Son makes you free, you shall be free indeed." (John 8:36) And "the blood of Jesus Christ His Son cleanses us from all sin." (1 John 1:7)

We all would do some things differently if we could live them over, but along the way we know we have matured in the Lord. We live under the Instructions given in Philippians 4:6-7: Be anxious for nothing, but in everything by prayer and supplication, with thanksgiving, let your requests be made known to God; and the peace of God, which surpasses all understanding, will guard your hearts and minds through Christ Jesus.

As we mature, we come to understand that "to be spiritually minded is life and peace." (Rom 8:6)

Now it is time for us to protect the younger generation from the wily serpent's methods. We are a model to the younger generation of what it means to live in "life and peace," instead of living for oneself.

As a spiritual father Paul had something else working through him--miracles.

Now God worked unusual miracles by the hands of Paul, so that even handkerchiefs or aprons were brought from his body to the sick, and the diseases left them and the evil spirits went out of them. (Acts 19:11-13)

We are part of the lineage that Paul helped create as one of the early-church spiritual fathers. The miracles that happened at his hands happen through us. Paul, as a spiritual father, modeled how to live. Have we ever had miracles in our own lives? Have we ever known someone who was healed? Have we ever prayed and seen God answer our prayers? Yes. God works through us. We embrace it. It is part of our own spiritual heritage, passed down to us.

Moreover, we get to pass it down to future generations. Second Timothy 1:7 says, "For God has not given us a spirit of fear, but of power and of love and of a sound mind."

We can analyze the operations of the gifts of the Spirit. We can theologically debate who has and who does not have the gift of the "working of miracles" that First Corinthians 12:10 talks about. Or we can declare that we are the heritage of the LORD and that He is equipping us for Kingdom work.

God is calling us to take our place as the "blessing" generation. Our spoken blessing changes the future generation as we declare blessings over them. We spiritual parents speak, and we see the Holy Spirit confirm the word with miracles in their lives. The truth is the younger generation can't make it without us. The Bible gives a very clear example of this in Exodus 17:8-13. Moses has led the children of Israel out of Egypt, but he is too old to lead them in battle. Instead he directs his spiritual son to lead the fight. The story goes like this:

> Now Amalek came and fought with Israel in Rephidim. And Moses said to Joshua, "Choose us some men and go out, fight with Amalek. Tomorrow I will stand on the top of the hill with the rod of God in my hand." So Joshua did as Moses said to him, and fought with Amalek. And Moses, Aaron, and Hur went up to the top of the hill. And so it was, when Moses held up his hand, that Israel prevailed; and when he let down his hand, Amalek prevailed. But Moses' hands became heavy; so they took a stone and put it under him, and he sat on it. And Aaron and Hur supported his hands, one on one side, and the other on the other side; and his hands were steady until the going down of the sun. So Joshua defeated Amalek and his people with the edge of the sword.

Like Moses, we 50+ers may not have the strength and energy of the younger generation, but we know how to connect with the Father! The younger generation wins as we guide them and call God's blessing on their lives and actions.

God is calling our generation to take our position. We, like Moses and Joshua, will see the enemy defeated. We are going to speak generational blessings over the next generation, connecting us as the heritage of the LORD.

HOW TO GIVE
GENERATIONAL BLESSINGS

"The LORD bless you and keep you; the LORD make His face shine upon you, and be gracious to you; the LORD lift up His countenance upon you, and give you peace." (Num 6:24-26)

One of the easiest, most rewarding, and most refreshing things we get to do as fathers and mothers in the LORD is to declare a blessing over the younger generation and others.

We 50+ers at MorningStar fellowship church have the privilege of declaring individual blessings over the students of our k-12 school and over the students at MorningStar University. We also declare generational blessings over attendees of all ages at MorningStar conferences. Most of them have never had a blessing declared over them. Every time we conduct these blessings, we are blessed back.

Here is an unsolicited response from a father of a family one of the 50+ teams blessed at a recent MorningStar conference:

I wanted to take the opportunity to tell you how amazing our experience was during our Generational Blessing ministry time. My wife, two children, and I didn't know what to expect.

We were greeted with such an amazing amount of love, gentleness, and youthful excitement. It seems as if they did not miss any area of our lives. I could feel the weight of past/present victories pressing into our lives and being shared with us. We were so surprised at the power released from the 50+ers.

Two days later, I still feel its effects. Again, the love we felt was quite amazing. Three 50+ers in a team had discovered a lifetime of the goodness of God and were desperate to share it with us. I don't even understand how to sum up such a gift.

Thank you for providing this experience. And please share with the 50+ group our joy of receiving it.

In the past, our generation was sometimes labeled "the silent majority." But no more. We will not be silent. We will speak blessings that change lives and circumstances.

Spoken words have power! We have all felt the sting of cruel words. We have all felt the life-changing impact of affirming words. I think back to the time in my teenage years when I finally got up the courage to tell a girl I loved her. I couldn't even say the words. I squeezed her hand three times instead. Even in my adolescence, I knew spoken words had power.

God our Father spoke the world into existence. He then spoke a blessing over us, His created beings:

So God created man in His own image; in the image of God He created him; male and female He created them. Then God blessed them, and God said to them, "Be fruitful and multiply; fill the earth and subdue it; have dominion over the fish of the sea, over the birds of the air, and over every living thing that moves on the earth." (Gen 1:27-28)

What He spoke over us came to pass. Now, many generations later, we as fathers and mothers in the Lord speak blessings over the younger generation as well.

Blessings aren't only from parents to children.

Jesus blessed his followers, us, as he ascended to heaven, as Luke 24:50-52 records: And He led them out as far as Bethany, and He lifted up His hands and blessed them. Now it came to pass, while He blessed them, that He was parted from them and carried up into heaven.

Rebekah's brothers, not her father, blessed her when she departed with Abraham's servant to become Isaac's wife. The story goes like this:

So they sent away Rebekah their sister and her nurse, and Abraham's servant and his men. And they blessed Rebekah and said to her: "Our sister, may you become the mother of thousands of ten thousands; and may your descendants possess the gates of those who hate them." (Gen 24:59-60)

The blessing they declared became a reality. From Rebekah came Jacob and Esau and their lineages of millions and millions. We are brothers and sisters in the Lord to younger Christians and can bless them also.

A blessing is a declaration. It speaks God's provision over the person. John Kilpatrick, who was instrumental in the Pensacola outpouring, says prayer, blessing, and prophecy are three different things.

Keep the distinction in mind. You don't pray a blessing over the individual; you simply speak it over the individual.

Blessing started with God who blessed mankind, saying "be fruitful and multiply." The patriarchs blessed their offspring. David blessed his household. Jesus blessed His followers as he ascended to heaven! As spiritual parents or seasoned spiritual warriors, we have the honor of blessing future generations, continuing the Godly connection from generation to generation, uniting, us the family of God, under His care.

GUIDELINES FOR ADMINISTERING GENERATIONAL BLESSINGS

Below are the guidelines that the 50+ Blessing Generation group at MorningStar Fellowship Church follows. We conduct generational blessings over conference attendees as well as students and others within the church.

1. At MorningStar we want a male and female team to administer the blessing over an individual.

2. The generational blessing can be to a person of any age.

3. The blessing (and any follow up prayer or comments) should take no more than 5 or 6 minutes, especially when there are many others waiting.

4. Realize that the Holy Spirit will be making the blessing alive and life changing to them, even if the blessing sounds simple or general.

5. Start by finding out the person's name and also introduce yourselves.

6. Explain the importance of a blessing and its use throughout the Bible.

   a. Let them know that you stand in as spiritual parents or the father and mother generation in the Lord to cover them and to acknowledge that forever they are in the spiritual lineage established by God in the very beginning of creation. You could say something like:

      i. Proverbs 18:21 says, "Death and life are in the power of the tongue." We speak life over you. Our blessing speaks life to you.

     ii. God created mankind by the words of his mouth, and then He blessed mankind. Genesis 1:27-28 says, "So God created man in His own image; in the image of God He created him; male and female He created them. Then God blessed them, and God said to them, 'Be fruitful and multiply; fill the earth and subdue it; have dominion over the fish of the sea, over the birds of the air, and over every living thing that moves on the earth.'"

   iii. The patriarchs blessed their offspring.

   iv. Jesus blessed his followers as he ascended to heaven, as Luke 24:51-52 records!

7. Ask permission to place your hand on the person's head to speak a blessing if you are going to touch them.

8. Tell them to keep their eyes open. You also keep your eyes open. Look right into their eyes. Their spirits open wide to your words when you look into their eyes.

9. Speak the blessing to them.

    a. You may even speak a blessing scripture over them such as Numbers 6:22-27 and use their name in the blessing.

    b. Speak out the declaration of who they are in the Lord and the calling, protection, and favor they have. Speak fullness and provision into their futures.

    c. You will discover that the blessing you speak over them may have prophetic elements that come through. But don't turn the blessing into an extended prophetic word that loses the focus of the blessing declaration. We don't want to dilute the blessing itself. The blessing itself is the main thing and will make what we do a uniquely significant touch point in their lives!

10. When you complete the blessing, remind the person that she (or he) is now sealed as a daughter of a loving Heavenly Father. She lives a Kingdom life under the Father's authority. She is not an orphan but a member of the family of God, and we blessers are a brother and sister in the body of Christ, her father and mother in the Lord. No matter what happens in the world, she is part of the Kingdom and will live under the Father's authority.

God is calling us, all of us, to enter the fullness of our lives right now, not just at MorningStar, but everywhere we 50+ers live. He isn't finished with us. He's renewing us. He's using us. Our best days are right now.

Organizing "blessers"

You understand the power of blessing. Now help others your age step into the same 50+ calling. Do a generational blessing over another 50+er. You will recognize the power in the blessing. Then get other 50+ers involved. Work as teams in your church and bless others, normally having a man and a woman for each team.

You may even bless your pastor. You have the spiritual authority needed to do this. You will change many lives, bringing spiritual orphans back to recognition of who they really are and preparing a younger generation to walk boldly in their spiritual destinies.

Blessing others isn't an option. It is part of our calling.

THE POWER OF A
SPIRITUAL LEGACY

"…The accuser of our brethren, who accused them before our God day and night, has been cast down. And they overcame him by the blood of the Lamb and by the word of their testimony…" (Rev 12:10-11)

He's sitting across from me at the kitchen table. Ten feet from us, cardinals and doves eat at my bird feeder by my back deck. John and I watch them. They can't see us because I have sun-reflecting film on my windows. We both like the birds. They remind us of our times in nature over the years.

Then John shares something with me that pulls my attention away from the birds, and, quite frankly, away from everything else. John is 85 and has lived a lot of life. He has stories to tell. He has told me about how he worked with Tom Brokaw before anybody had heard of Tom Brokaw. He's told me about building a radio station and being an administrator in colleges. He and his wife have traveled around the world in significant missions and spiritual restitution work. All of his stories are good. He speaks in a relaxed voice and a broad smile much of the time. I'm ready for another story. This one is different, though. It's a spiritual legacy story. And he has my full attention instantly.

"I was in Waynesville, North Carolina," he starts, with the same relaxed voice and ready smile that is so much his personality. "I was outside, thinking of the ministry I was handling and all I had to do as the administrator. Then I heard a voice say, 'I'm more interested in who you are and who you're becoming than in what you're doing.'"

When John says this, he smiles at me and continues. "'What?' I said. 'That can't be right. God is certainly interested in what I'm doing. I'm building this ministry.' But it kept coming back to me, 'I'm more interested in who you are than in what you're doing.'

"'I'm more interested in who you are and what you're doing? I rebuke that in the name of Jesus,' I said." Now John laughs one of his winning laughs, and I can't help but smile back. He continues.

"That makes no sense to me. Obviously the Lord is interested in what I'm doing, I thought. 'Lord, if this is really you, I need a little help. Give me some input.'"

Then John says to me, "I don't know about you, but often the Lord doesn't explain himself a lot to us."

He goes on, "That was the beginning of a journey. If what I heard was true, I had to see it in Scripture.

"We all know Romans 8:28, 'All things work together for good to those who love God and are called according to his purpose.' The next verse goes on to say, 'For those he foreknew, He also predestined to be conformed to the image of His Son.' ...So, in the ordinary vernacular, what the Lord is really saying is, 'I want you to be like Jesus.' To become like Jesus... It's an ongoing process.

"He's very interested in what we're doing, obviously. If we have a part in building something for the Kingdom, He's interested in that. And if He's even more interested in who we're becoming, then, wow, I need to change my emphasis. ', I want to become more like You.'"

John continues his story for a few minutes. But I already have the point. He's sharing a spiritual legacy story without even realizing it.

I few days later the Christmas intergenerational party takes place. About 150 MorningStar Church Blessing Generation 50+ers and MorningStar University students are together to love each other and celebrate before the students leave on their Christmas break. I ask John to share his story. As he does, I can see the eyes of some of the students, and even their leaders, get a little larger and start to water up a little. The Holy Spirit is using the story to bring home an important truth to this younger generation.

John's not preaching. He's not even teaching. He's just sharing a spiritual life experience. And it is making an impact. That's what spiritual legacy stories do. They touch the next generation. They guide our children and grandchildren. Future generations hear of God's faithfulness.

After John shares, I get an idea, "This year when I go up North for Christmas, I'm going to have a few of these spiritual legacy stories ready to share with my grandkids when I tuck them in bed. They love to hear my stories, anyway. I am going to be more intentional."

I did. And it had an impact.

We are living letters, as Paul describes to the Corinthians:

You yourselves are our letter, written on our hearts, known and read by everybody. You show that you are a letter from Christ, the result of our ministry, written not with ink but with the Spirit of the living God, not on tablets of stone but on tablets of human hearts. (2 Cor 3:3, NIV)

Others read us. Future generations are interested in us. They need us and are looking for guidance. In a generation where the social media dominates superficial communication, our stories make a much more powerful connection.

Our stories are our testimony. Don't underestimate their importance. We overcome the accuser of the brethren and block his authority over our children and future generations.

We as spiritual fathers and mothers bless the Lord and praise His works to the next generation. We as blessers in the Joshua and Caleb generation stand in the gap, linking the past to future generations that they may understand the beauty, power, and faithfulness of the Lord and thus desire to love and obey Him.

The psalmist describes it this way:

I will extol You, my God, O King; and I will bless Your name forever and ever. Every day I will bless You, and I will praise Your name forever and ever. Great is the LORD, and greatly to be praised; and His greatness is unsearchable. One generation shall praise Your works to another, and shall declare Your mighty acts....

All Your works shall praise You, O LORD, and Your saints shall bless You. They shall speak of the glory of Your kingdom, and talk of Your power, to make known to the sons of men His mighty acts, and the glorious majesty of His kingdom. (Ps 145:1-4, 10-12)

Psalms 78:1-6 explains the process established by God for his people:

Give ear, O my people, to my law; incline your ears to the words of my mouth. I will open my mouth in a parable; I will utter dark sayings of old, which we have heard and known, and our fathers have told us. We will not hide them from their children, telling to the generation to come the praises of the LORD, and His strength and His wonderful works that He has done.

For He established a testimony in Jacob, and appointed a law in Israel, which He commanded our fathers, that they should make them known to their children; that the generation to come might know them, the children who would be born, that they may arise and declare them to their children,

Then Psalms 78:7 explains the result:

That they (future generations) may set their hope in God, and not forget the works of God, but keep His commandments.

By the time we get to be our age, we have many stories we can tell. But how do we do it? And who will listen? The answer to the first question is: we will do it easily. The answer to the second is: you will be surprised at the number of people who will be touched by the Holy Spirit when they hear or read a spiritual legacy story you share.

The apostle John tells us in 1 John 1:1-4,

That which was from the beginning, which we have heard, which we have seen with our eyes, which we have looked upon, and our hands have handled, concerning the Word of life...we declare to you, that you also may have fellowship with us.

Two things about this passage stand out as part of the importance of spiritual legacies.

First of all, Jesus shared himself with his disciples. He told stories and experiences to others as a main way of communicating. Those stories impacted John the apostle when he heard them. We are like Christ, sharing ourselves, too.

Secondly, now John is going to share the spiritual legacy. He is, in essence, often telling us about spiritual encounters with the Lord. The Gospel of John is filled with remarkable stories about Jesus' interactions with John and others disciples.

The apostle Paul declares us to be living letters for others to read. He says,

You are our epistle written in our hearts, known and read by all men; clearly you are an epistle of Christ, ministered by us, written not with ink but by the Spirit of the living God, not on tablets of stone but on the tablets of flesh, that is, the heart. (2 Cor 3:2-3)

Imagine that. We are living letters, walking around for others to read. So, why not share our stories with others who can't physically be in our presence? The spiritual legacy stories we tell in person, write for others to read, record for others to listen to, or video for others to see will convey that each of us is an "epistle (a letter) of Christ." They will recognize the Spirit's impact.

Let me repeat the verses from the opening of this chapter:

*Then I heard a loud voice saying in heaven, 'Now salvation, and strength, and the kingdom of our God, and the power of His Christ have come, for the accuser of our brethren, who accused them before God day and night, has been cast down. And they overcame him by the blood of the lamb **and by the word of their testimony**, and they did not love their lives to the death.' (Rev 12:10-11 NKJV, emphasis mine)*

An important weapon coming against Satan and overcoming him is the word of our testimony. We proclaim the mighty acts of God in our lives to others. It's not that we should consider doing this if we have the time; it's that we must do this to help cast down "the accuser of the brethren." Our spiritual legacies have more power than we imagine.

We have the power of Christ within us that we release through the testimonies of what He has done in our lives. First John 4:4 says,

> *You are of God little children, and have overcome them (spirit of the antichrist), because He who is in you is greater than he who is in the world.*

The stories of God's power, faithfulness, and provision that we release are in direct contrast to the religiosity we have lived through in America for the past 40 years or more. The stories break through the religious spirit that is prevalent today, that spirit of antichrist that counterfeits the acts of Holy Spirit--because greater is He who is in us than he who is in the world.

We are entering a critical time on God's clock. The harvest is going to be great. Our stories will help usher in the next "Great Awakening" that has been prophesied.

Also, we can't allow the younger generation to walk through the same circumstances we've had to endure. We would not be advancing the Kingdom. We want to instill spiritual courage and a deepened faith in them right now so that they will be able to be overcomers, even as darkening events surround their lives. They will walk in the light and cast out darkness because the simple spiritual legacy stories we've shared with them equip them in ways only the Father knows.

We are the true emerging generation, stepping into our calling, covering future generations and leading them to their "promised land."

So now, what qualifies you to leave a spiritual legacy? After all, you've had sin in your life in the past. You've failed at times, even though God picked you back up. You've been confused at times, not knowing what path to take or who to marry or what church to go to or what job to apply for and on and on.

All of that uniquely qualifies you to share your experiences. You've been there. You can tell how God forgave your mistakes. You can tell how God was faithful to you when you were down to your last dollar. You can tell how God whispered a warning in your mind that prevented an accident from happening. You have many stories to tell. They're in there, waiting to burst forth in life for others who need to hear or read them.

You've matured. You realize it is not about you. You're not trying to get center stage and be recognized. It's about something much bigger than that. It's about seeing God's kingdom come into others' lives as He has also come into your life. If Saul of Tarsus, who murdered Christians, is qualified to bring Kingdom life, you are qualified!

"But I don't have the skills needed to create a spiritual legacy," you might be thinking. Well, my answer to that is that the only "skill" you need is that of breathing. You tell stories of experiences in your life all the time. At the end of the day you may share the day's events (stories of what happened during the day) with your spouse. Or, when you go to someone's home, you all shares stories of what has been happening in your life lately.

You're telling stories every day. Now all you have to do is be a little more intentional. You have a spiritual legacy to release that will bring God into the lives of those around you.

A spiritual legacy is counter-cultural. Our 50+ generation may be the last generation that had deep relationships in the home. In the '60s and '70s young adults and others rebelled against the traditional family structure. Spiritual war on the family went to a new level. Financial success during a period of growth in America became a driver that pulled fathers from family life. TV ended the family dinner in many homes. Remember the "tv dinners" we used to buy so we could watch TV and eat at the same time? Then the Internet developed, allowing the younger generation to have virtual relationships that were a poor substitute for the love and relationships that they never encountered growing up.

But we 50+ers are declaring an end to the estrangement and separation between the generations. We are restoring generational connections. In the same way the spiritual legacy stories the Israelites told gave their offspring a focus on God rather than on the hedonism and self-worship around them, our stories will refocus future generations on the God Who loves them.

The next chapter will help you recall spiritual legacies that will have an impact on future generations.

CREATING YOUR SPIRITUAL LEGACY

SPIRITUAL LEGACY MISSION STATEMENT

We will declare God's faithfulness, power, and provision to future generations, that they too may know and live in God's love and purpose.

Review the mission statement above. Keep it as a focus of each spiritual legacy story you create. You are going to have fun working through this chapter. The Holy Spirit will quicken stories and memories. You may find yourself getting emotional at times as you recall how God intervened at a crucial moment or as you recognize God's leading or healing.

Although you can use this chapter for creating your personal spiritual legacy, I recommend that you actually get a group of 50+ers together to do the exercises and then to share with each other. You will all be encouraged, and their stories may trigger even more spiritual legacy stories for you.

As you will discover when you work through the different exercises in this chapter, you can take one or two exercises a week and create some spiritual legacies. Then you can meet with your 50+ group and share the stories. An added benefit is that members can share their skills with each other. Perhaps one person is really good on a computer and can help others. Often there is a person who likes videoing. That person can video the stories.

In the Appendix I talk about ways of permanently capturing spiritual legacy stories--written, audio, video, YouTube, etc. You will find the information useful. But first, let's find spiritual legacy stories from our own lives.

Every day I hear spiritual legacy stories from the 50+ers I pastor as we talk. I have to remind them that they just shared a spiritual legacy story that they can pass on to future generations.

You may want a pen or computer handy as you work through this chapter. I have put a Notes Page after each separate Spiritual Legacy idea. The Holy Spirit will trigger some story ideas. Write them down. You can even outline a few points about the story so you will remember what to expand upon later.

Don't rush. Perhaps only do one idea a day or one idea a week. You will discover that you will not have a shortage of stories to share.

Before you start creating these spiritual legacy stories, read the following spiritual legacy scriptures. They will confirm to you that you are doing exactly what God loves for you to do.

SPIRITUAL LEGACY SCRIPTURES

"I will open my mouth in a parable; I will utter dark sayings of old, which we have heard and known, and our fathers have told us. We will not hide them from their children, telling to the generation to come the praises of

the LORD, and His strength and His wonderful works that He has done.

"For He established a testimony in Jacob, and appointed a law in Israel, which He commanded our fathers, that they should make them known to their children; that the generation to come might know them, the children who would be born, that they may arise and declare them to their children." (Ps 78:2-6)

"This will be written for the generation to come, that a people yet to be created may praise the LORD." (Ps 102:18)

"Seek the LORD and His strength; seek His face evermore! Remember His marvelous works which He has done, His wonders, and the judgments of His mouth, O seed of Israel His servant, You children of Jacob, His chosen ones!

"He is the LORD our God; His judgments are in all the earth. Remember His covenant forever, the word which He commanded, for a thousand generations...." (1 Chron 16:11-15)--We are part of that thousand generations. First Chronicles 16:1-36 is David's great psalm in front of the people, praising the LORD for all He has done.

"So we, Your people and sheep of Your pasture, will give You thanks forever; we will show forth Your praise to all generations." (Ps 79:13)

"I will sing of the mercies of the LORD forever; with my mouth will I make known Your faithfulness to all generations." (Ps 89:1)

*"Enter into His gates with thanksgiving, And into His courts with praise. Be thankful to Him, and bless His name. For the L*ORD* is good; His mercy is everlasting, and His truth endures to all generations." (Ps 100:4-5)*

*"Forever, O L*ORD*, Your word is settled in heaven. Your faithfulness endures to all generations; You established the earth, and it abides." (Ps 119:89-90)*

*"I will extol You, my God, O King; and I will bless Your name forever and ever. Every day I will bless You, and I will praise Your name forever and ever. Great is the L*ORD*, and greatly to be praised; and His greatness is unsearchable. One generation shall praise Your works to another, and shall declare Your mighty acts.*

*"All Your works shall praise You, O L*ORD*, and Your saints shall bless You. They shall speak of the glory of Your kingdom, and talk of Your power, to make known to the sons of men His mighty acts, and the glorious majesty of His kingdom. Your kingdom is an everlasting kingdom, and Your dominion endures throughout all generations." (Ps 145:1-4, 10-13)*

"Now to Him who is able to do exceedingly abundantly above all that we ask or think, according to the power that works in us, to Him be glory in the church by Christ Jesus to all generations, forever and ever." (Eph 3:20-21)

Now it's your turn to release the spiritual legacies in your life. The following exercises will help.

Discoveries: Seeking, Pursuing, Finding

"But seek first the kingdom of God and His righteousness, and all these things shall be added to you. Therefore do not worry about tomorrow, for tomorrow will worry about its own things." (Matt 6:33-34)

"But without faith it is impossible to please Him, for he who comes to God must believe that He is, and that He is a rewarder of those who diligently seek Him." (Heb 11:6)

"Who can find a virtuous wife? For her worth is far above rubies. The heart of her husband safely trusts her; so he will have no lack of gain." (Pr 31:10)

"But you, O man of God,...pursue righteousness, godliness, faith, love, patience, gentleness." (1 Tim 6:11)

Instructions:

What are some things you pursued that led you to a good outcome? What are some discoveries along the way that would be good to let a future generation know about?

Why did you pursue certain things? How did you do it? What was the result when you finally got it? What did you finally discover?

Think about a time you pursued or found or discovered something of significance that was God-assisted.

Legacy includes pursuing—
   » God
   » Your dreams
   » A purpose
   » A destiny

» The Kingdom

Legacy stories include finding/discovering —
» Peace
» Purpose
» God
» Spiritual rest
» A mate
» A Godly heritage
» Joy
» Fulfillment

(Remember, don't preach. Simply share a personal incident and how it impacted you.)

NOTES PAGE

"Righting" the Story of Your Life

"Now it came to pass in those days, when Moses was grown, that he went out to his brethren and looked at their burdens. And he saw an Egyptian beating a Hebrew, one of his brethren. So he looked this way and that way, and when he saw no one, he killed the Egyptian and hid him in the sand." (Ex 2:11-13)

"Peter said to Him, 'Lord, why can I not follow You now? I will lay down my life for Your sake.' Jesus answered him, 'Will you lay down your life for My sake? Most assuredly, I say to you, the rooster shall not crow till you have denied Me three times.'" (John 13:37-38)

"For I know that in me (that is, in my flesh) nothing good dwells; for to will is present with me, but how to perform what is good I do not find.... There is therefore now no condemnation to those who are in Christ Jesus, who do not walk according to the flesh, but according to the Spirit. For the law of the Spirit of life in Christ Jesus has made me free from the law of sin and death." (Rom 7:18-19; 8:1-3)

Instructions

Are there chapters of your life you would like to edit if you could? Do over? Do more? Do better? Do differently? Have fear, shame, regret, or guilt been a companion in those places? You're in good company.

Rick Joyner thought back over some of the mistakes and fumbles he had made in his ministry and felt badly. Later, the Lord spoke to him about his mistakes. Rick paraphrased what the Lord said as follows:

All of the fumbles and mistakes are to prepare us for what is coming. Soon we will play on a much bigger stage, for much higher stakes, and all of our previous mistakes will enable us to help carry what will be entrusted to us without fumbling.[3]

Think of some of the mistakes and fumbles you've made. What were they? But, more importantly, what have you learned? If you are like me, you have a few spiritual legacy stories to tell here. Tell each story frankly. A future generation will learn and not have to walk through the same things.

---

3 Morningstar Partners Monthly Newsletter, May, 2012.

NOTES PAGE

Your Scriptural History

"Then Jacob was left alone; and a Man wrestled with him until the breaking of day. Now when He saw that He did not prevail against him, He touched the socket of his hip; and the socket of Jacob's hip was out of joint as He wrestled with him. And He said, 'Let Me go, for the day breaks.' But he said, 'I will not let You go unless You bless me!'" (Gen. 32:24-26)

"Then Elijah said to Ahab, 'Go up, eat and drink; for there is the sound of abundance of rain.' So Ahab went up to eat and drink. And Elijah went up to the top of Carmel; then he bowed down on the ground, and put his face between his knees, and said to his servant, 'Go up now, look toward the sea.' So he went up and looked, and said, 'There is nothing.' And seven times he said, 'Go again.' Then it came to pass the seventh time, that he said, 'There is a cloud, as small as a man's hand, rising out of the sea!' So he said, 'Go up, say to Ahab, 'Prepare your chariot, and go down before the rain stops you.'' Now it happened in the meantime that the sky became black with clouds and wind, and there was a heavy rain. So Ahab rode away and went to Jezreel." (1 Kings 18:41-45)

Instructions

When you look back over your life, both in crises and successes, where in the Word has God met you—even those times when like Jacob you may have wrestled with God? How were you changed?

List those Scriptures where the life you surrendered was "altared" by fire. This is your personal Scriptural history, the Word, made flesh in Christ and now in you.

There are times when the *logos*, the inspired Word of God, becomes *rhema*, the utterance of God specifically to you, i.e., a verse or a portion of Scripture that the Holy Spirit brings to your attention with application to a current situation or need for direction.

Tell of a time when God brought *rhema* to your situation.

NOTES PAGE

Organizing your spiritual legacy

Now that you've started capturing some spiritual legacies, you may want to think how to organize them. The following exercise, "Remembrance over the Decades," can help you. It is especially good if you are working on a family history (in which, of course, you include spiritual legacy stories) or want to tell your stories chronologically.

You will see the Instructions for the exercise itself. Then you will see my personal example from when I was doing this with other 50+ers. Then there is a blank form that you can also write on. Or you can do this simply on your computer. I have also included a Notes Page to add further thoughts.

Remembrance over the Decades

"Bless the LORD, *O my soul, and forget not all His benefits."* *(Ps 103:2)*

"Then those who feared the LORD *spoke to one another, and the* LORD *listened and heard them; So a book of remembrance was written before Him for those who fear the* LORD *and who meditate on His name." (Mal 3:16)*

"Incline your ears to the words of my mouth. I will open my mouth in a parable; I will utter dark sayings of old, which we have heard and known, and our fathers have told us. We will not hide them from their children, telling to the generation to come the praises of the LORD, *and His strength and His wonderful works that He has done." (Ps 78:1-4)*

Instructions

Look back over your life and remember and write down, if you've not already, what the Lord has done for you and through you. ("Remember" and "remembrance" are referenced 200 times in the Bible. Must be important to God!)

Perhaps start with the present decade and work backwards, showing to the person(s) you've dedicated this legacy, God's faithfulness. Or perhaps you can work forward through the decades, explaining how God was there.

Choose at least one example to develop from one of the time periods. You can add more examples as you continue to work on spiritual legacies. **Define what the decade meant in your life. This will help recall specific spiritual legacy stories.**

119

"Remembrance over the Decades" example
John Boneck personal example:

2010 to the present
Loss, grieving, renewal, and walking in God's calling

2000 - 2009
Transitions

1990-1999
Laboring in hope; prophetic dream

1980 - 1989
Establishing a future

1970 - 1979

The Holy Spirit and A family

Barb and I were powerfully impacted by the Holy Spirit in 1972 when we were in school in Colorado. It became part of a revival in the church we attended.

We moved to California where Barb almost died within three weeks of arriving there. The baby she was carrying died within her and poisoned her. After that we did not know if she could have a child. She had two more miscarriages. After the last one, I left the hospital and went home and cried. I opened the Bible as I lay on the bed and a scripture about a man child being born popped out at me. (There are several references in the King James version of the Bible. I don't remember which one it is.) I felt the Holy Spirit was promising a child to Barbara and me. The next pregnancy was totally normal, and Carson was born. After that Barb had another miscarriage, and we recognized that Carson was to be the only child we would have.

One of the verses that God gave to me when I was saddened by our circumstances is: I will instruct you and teach you in the way you should go; I will guide you with My eye. (Ps 32:8) It has become one of my life verses.

1960 - 1969
Becoming a man in marriage and employment

1950-1959
Good childhood but loss of father. Then surrogate dads in church and all the time with a praying mother.

1944 - 1949
With mom and dad.

"REMEMBRANCE OVER THE DECADES" FORM

2010 to the present

2000 – 2009

1990-1999

1980 - 1989

1970 - 1979

1960 - 1969

1950-1959

1940 - 1949

1930 - 1939

NOTES PAGE

Great Life Events

"But the angel said to him, 'Do not be afraid, Zacharias, for your prayer is heard; and your wife Elizabeth will bear you a son, and you shall call his name John. And you will have joy and gladness, and many will rejoice at his birth.'" (Luke 1:13-14)

"Let him kiss me with the kisses of his mouth — for your love is better than wine." (Song of Sol 1:2)

"Now as for you, you shall go to your fathers in peace; you shall be buried at a good old age." (Gen 15:15)

Instructions

We remember life's big events and often tell stories and reminisce to friends. Think of a significant life event and consider how God was in it. He is in our significant events in big and little ways. He cares about every detail of our lives. Tell a story of God in a significant event. You don't have to tell about the entire event. Instead focus on God's hand or leading or direction in the event. It may be that you look back and recognize that God was actually orchestrating some things you did not realize at the time. Great life events can include —

- » Births
- » Falling in love
- » Marriage
- » Death
- » Moving — location
- » Fulfillment of your desire for: vocation, mate, purpose, calling, etc.

NOTES PAGE

The Power of Two

"Two are better off than one, because together they can work more effectively. If one of them falls down, the other can help him up... Two people can resist an attack that would defeat one person alone. A rope made of three cords is hard to break."(Ecclesiastes 4:9, 10, 12, TEV)

"Two are better than one, because they have a good reward for their labor. For if they fall, one will lift up his companion. But woe to him who is alone when he falls, for he has no one to help him up. Again, if two lie down together, they will keep warm; but how can one be warm alone? Though one may be overpowered by another, two can withstand him. And a threefold cord is not quickly broken."(Ecclesiastes 4:9-12)

Instructions

This exercise involves your "best friend."

At certain stages of our lives, different very special friends may appear. You may have had someone who became a special counselor or guide to you when you were younger and needed someone to understand. You may have moved to a different area and established some very special friendship in your new surroundings. Think about that special friend or friends and write how God has used that relationship. Why is it so important to have deep, quality relationships?

The younger generation may not understand the power of relationship. What can they learn from what you shared?

Take time to write, video, or record how God has used a "best friend" in your life.

You might want to mention the risks and rewards of desiring a best friend.

Risks—Betrayal, Vulnerability, Loss of the friend

Rewards—Confidante, Support, Balance in your life, Love, Joy, Adventure, Sounding board-counselor, Companionship, They help you grow, Strength from the relationship of two, Iron sharpens iron, Help

NOTES PAGE

Values

"Behold, You desire truth in the inward parts, and in the hidden part You will make me to know wisdom." (Ps 51:6)

"Justice is turned back, and righteousness stands afar off; for truth is fallen in the street, and equity cannot enter. So truth fails, and he who departs from evil makes himself a prey.

"Then the LORD saw it, and it displeased Him that there is no justice." (Isa 59:14-15)

"Pilate said to Him, 'What is truth?'" (John 18:38)

Instructions

Our values are the foundation for our decisions.

What values did you discover along the way, how did you discover them, what are the results of walking in them, what are the consequences of not walking in them?

Examples of values:
- » Honesty
- » Integrity
- » Fidelity
- » Humility
- » Perseverance
- » Forgiveness
- » Love
- » Hope
- » The benefit of working hard
- » Surrender to God

» Understanding your position as a son/daughter of the Father

Is there a story you can tell about a time you discovered the importance of maintaining Godly values?

NOTES PAGE

Overcoming and Breakthrough

"He who overcomes shall inherit all things, and I will be his God and he shall be my son." (Rev 21:7)

Instructions

God's children are called overcomers in the Word. We have overcome many things. And each time we overcome, we are bringing the Kingdom of God into the situation. We are defeating Satan's purposes and plans.

Below are some possible areas you have been an overcomer.
- » Overcoming fear
- » Overcoming anxiety
- » Overcoming insecurity
- » Overcoming anger
- » Overcoming the ordinary to pursue your God dream
- » Overcoming feeling unworthy
- » Overcoming being hurt or wounded by someone

Tell a story of an incident in your overcoming life. What were the circumstances that contributed to the need to overcome? How did the overcoming occur? What were the results?

Spiritual legacies include breakthroughs also.

Breakthroughs can include —
- » When others didn't understand you
- » When you didn't know what to do
- » When you had been hurt or lost someone you loved
- » When you had little or no money
- » When you needed a job

» When you experienced a crisis in your family
» When a seemingly insurmountable obstacle was in your path

How did you break through to the other side of the problem? How was God involved? What did you learn?

NOTES PAGE

God's "Language"

"The heavens declare the glory of God; and the firmament shows His handiwork. Day unto day utters speech, and night unto night reveals knowledge. There is no speech nor language where their voice is not heard." (Ps 19:1-3)

"And behold, the LORD passed by, and a great and strong wind tore into the mountains and broke the rocks in pieces before the LORD, but the LORD was not in the wind; and after the wind an earthquake, but the LORD was not in the earthquake; and after the earthquake a fire, but the LORD was not in the fire; and after the fire a still small voice." (1 Kings 19:11-12)

Instructions

God speaks to us in a language we can understand. Can you give an example of how the Lord speaks to you, i.e., what language does He use? How did He speak to you in a meaningful way at an important moment of your life in a "language" you understand?

Some of God's languages can include—
  » Nature
  » The arts—music, painting, architecture, dance, poetry, writing, etc.
  » Colors
  » Design
  » Pattern
  » Numbers
  » Coincidences
  » Humor
  » Opposites

» Satire

» Historical context

» Repetitions

» Voice — in your mind or actual

» Impressions

» The senses — smell, taste, touch, sight, hearing

» Prophetic word from someone

A younger generation may think a person only hears from God by reading the Bible or by listening to a sermon. A spiritual legacy story of how God "languaged" himself to you can open their understanding to hearing God the Father in new ways.

NOTES PAGE

Development

"And everyone who competes for the prize is temperate in all things. Now they do it to obtain a perishable crown, but we for an imperishable crown. Therefore I run thus: not with uncertainty. Thus I fight: not as one who beats the air. But I discipline my body and bring it into subjection...." (1 Cor 9:25-27)

"I have fought the good fight, I have finished the race, I have kept the faith." (2 Tim 4:7-8)

"And let the beauty of the LORD our God be upon us, And establish the work of our hands for us; Yes, establish the work of our hands." (Ps 90:17)

"Upon entering, Gabriel greeted her: Good morning! You're beautiful with God's beauty, Beautiful inside and out! God be with you." (Luke 1:28, THE MESSAGE: The Bible in Contemporary Language)

Instructions

John Eldredge writes in *Wild at Heart*, "...They may be misplaced, forgotten, or misdirected, but in the heart of every man is a desperate desire for a battle to fight, an adventure to live, and a beauty to rescue." [4]

Stasi Eldredge in *Captivating* writes, "...Every woman in her heart of hearts longs for three things: to be romanced, to play an irreplaceable role in a great adventure, and to unveil beauty."

As you develop your legacy, can you see the adventure

---

4 John Eldredge, *Wild at Heart* (Nashville, TN: Thomas Nelson, Nashville, TN, 2001), 9.

unfolded, the battle(s), the romance, the beauty? Can you also tell how love has made you better?

Can you create a spiritual legacy story from one of the following?
  » My greatest life adventure(s)…thus far
  » My greatest battle(s)…thus far
  » My romance(s)…thus far
  » My quest for and found beauty…thus far.

NOTES PAGE

Spiritual Legacy Potpourri

Instructions

You say you need a few more ideas for spiritual legacy stories? Okay, select any from the list below to use as a spiritual legacy story

Legacies include learning from mistakes. This shows you are human. People will relate to you.
- » What you learned from mistakes. How mistakes can be helpful.
- » How God puts a person back on the path
- » Mistakes are not fatal
- » We all have made mistakes

Legacies include contrasts and comparisons of old life to new life in Christ.
- » The difference between religion and God
- » How you changed when you encountered God
- » Old way of life vs. new life
- » Old way of thinking vs. new way of thinking
- » Your purpose and values before God versus your purpose and values after you met God
- » Love vs. Hate
- » Pride vs. Humility
- » Being vs. Doing

Legacies include God's active involvement in your life

- » How God helped bring your dream or goal to reality
- » God's faithfulness in catastrophes or tragedies
- » Miracles you have seen
- » Miracles that have happened to you

» How you felt forgiveness. How you found the power to forgive someone who had hurt you

» How you changed from the "gospel of salvation" type of life to "gospel of the Kingdom" type of life

» How you discovered God your Father really loves you

Legacies include God's guidance

» How to choose wise counselors; help from Godly counselors

» How you learned who to trust or not trust

» What you learned in wilderness experiences (and their importance)

» Knowing whether it is God's plan or your plan

» How you discovered how to make the right decisions

» How you discovered God's will

Legacies include your unique identity

» How God made you an introvert or extrovert

» How God made you creative or logical or sympathetic or systematic

» How God made you a happy or a serious person

» How God made you a thinker or a doer

» How God made you tall or short or large or small

» How God designed you in your ethnic or cultural identity

NOTES PAGE

Note: If you are creating a spiritual legacy book, this exercise could be a chapter idea.[5]

Life is...

Let this be recorded for future generations, so that a people not yet born will praise the LORD. *(Ps 102:18, Holy Bible, New Living Translation ®)*

Instructions

What will you write for your legacy to future generations? The following exercise will help you speak metaphorically.

1. Explain how God has been present in your life through a chosen metaphor. Finish the sentence, "**Life is...,** with your own metaphor.

Below are some examples of metaphors:
...**a test."**
...**a circus."**
...**a story."**
...**an adventure."**
...**a song to be sung."**
...**a race to run."**
...**a prize to be won."**
"**...like a box of chocolates. You never know what you're gonna get..." (Forrest Gump)**
...**about letting God use you for his purposes."**
...**other.**

---

5 Thanks to Trudy Goerk, who wrote this spiritual legacy idea and others.

2. Now, explain what you mean.

If your life is a song, what are the verses and the repeated chorus? If a story, what are the chapters you want to share? This is your outline, the skeleton bones that you will speak or write to bring your legacy to life.

NOTES PAGE

The Commanded Blessing

"So God created man in His own image; in the image of God He created him; male and female He created them. Then God blessed them, and God said to them, 'Be fruitful and multiply; fill the earth and subdue it; have dominion over the fish of the sea, over the birds of the air, and over every living thing that moves on the earth.'" (Gen 1:27-28)

"'The LORD bless you and keep you; The LORD make His face shine upon you, And be gracious to you; The LORD lift up His countenance upon you, and give you peace.' So they shall put My name on the children of Israel, and I will bless them." (Num 6:22-27)

"Behold, I will send you Elijah the prophet before the coming of the great and dreadful day of the LORD. And he will turn the hearts of the fathers to the children, and the hearts of the children to their fathers." (Mal 4:5-6)

"'For I, the LORD, I will direct their work in truth, and will make with them an everlasting covenant. Their descendants shall be known among the Gentiles, and their offspring among the people. All who see them shall acknowledge them, that they are the posterity whom the LORD has blessed.'" (Excerpts from Isaiah 61:5-11)

"And He (Jesus) led them out as far as Bethany, and He lifted up His hands and blessed them. Now it came to pass, while He blessed them, that He was parted from them and carried up into heaven. And they worshiped Him, and returned to Jerusalem with great joy, and

were continually in the temple praising and blessing God. Amen." (Luke 24:50-53) [That must have been some blessing.]

Instructions

One of the most important spiritual acts we as parents or seasoned spiritual warriors can perform is to bless our children and/or others who are in future generations. We speak a future of hope to them and connect them to the spiritual lineage established by God the Father when He first blessed Adam and Eve.

Write or video or record a blessing for one of your children or for a younger relative or for someone you know of a future generation.

Perhaps you want to write or video or record a blessing for future generations in your lineage yet unborn. You may want to speak the blessing directly to them now that you have created it.

You could even write or record a blessing for special events. For example, you could give your grandchildren or someone younger in the church a blessing at each birthday or at the start of each new year.

NOTES PAGE

NEXT STEPS

So we, Your people and sheep of Your pasture, will give You thanks forever; we will show forth Your praise to all generations. (Ps 79:13)

We will yet do exploits for the LORD. We will pray our grandchildren into the Kingdom. We will comfort those who mourn. We will supply finances for a Kingdom project. We will go on mission trips and touch other people's lives deeply. We will intercede for others when we are not mobile enough to be on the front lines ourselves. We will offer compassion to others. We will love, always love, someone else who needs love. We will love our next-door neighbor right into the Kingdom. We will be elders in the gates, sharing the wisdom of the Lord and bringing Godly knowledge to troubling circumstances. We will even influence and change nations. We are part of the army of the Lord. We look forward to victory. We are children of the Father, enjoying the bounty of Kingdom blessing and purpose. We are grateful.

We declare Galatians 2:20: I have been crucified with Christ; it is no longer I who live, but Christ lives in me; and the life which I now live in the flesh I live by faith in the Son of God, who loved me and gave Himself for me.

We are the Joshua and Caleb generation and will lead the next generation into their promised land, will share the stories of God's faithfulness, and will bless them in their kingdom walk.

From reading this book, write down some specific next steps you are going to take to walk fully in your calling.

One —

Two —

Three —

Four —

Appendix

The appendix is a mini-guide on ways to tell spiritual legacy stories and possible ways to present them to others. I will go in-depth in some areas and offer many types of suggestions. Simply take the portions that help you. Don't let the details scare you. Only take what you need.

TIPS FOR TELLING YOUR SPIRITUAL LEGACY STORY

"You are our epistle written in our hearts, known and read by all men; clearly you are an epistle of Christ, ministered by us, written not with ink but by the Spirit of the living God, not on tablets of stone but on the tablets of flesh, that is, the heart." (2 Cor 3:2-3)

Share your stories with other 50+ers

I recommend meeting with other 50+ers and working together to create spiritual legacy stories. I conducted some classes for the 50+ Blessing Generation group at Morning-Star Fellowship Church and had people share their stories with each other. It was powerful. As people sat around tables in small groups of 4 or 5 and shared their stories, others were deeply moved. They could feel the power of the Holy Spirit during what the person thought was simply a story of something God had done in his or her life.

You can work on one or two assignments a week from the

"Creating a Spiritual Legacy" chapter. You'll be surprised at the power in the stories.

When you work with groups, let everyone know they don't have to be writers. Some people are better at just writing down a few key ideas from a story so that they remember the story well. They can then just tell their stories during the table talk time when you are together.

You do not have to have a written spiritual legacy. For most of recorded history, stories were oral rather than written. The biggest thing is to share the stories of God's faithfulness in our lives to future generations.

Those who would rather tell their stories than write their stories will be able to share their stories with others during any conversation when the time is appropriate because they have prepared themselves for this remarkable privilege.

Tell your story

A spiritual legacy is nothing more complicated than telling a story to someone about something that happened. It comes from your personality and experience. Some of us think in terms of comparisons and the poetic. Some of us are matter of fact. We simply tell the story through our own personality.

Who are you telling your stories to?

Determine your audience. It will make a huge difference in how you tell the story, how complicated it can be, what facts you might want to add, etc.

Are you telling your story to your children? to relatives? to the younger generation in the church? to children yet unborn?

For example, perhaps you want to create some spiritual legacy stories for grandchildren. Then make the stories simple. Include things they will be interested in (How old were you then? Were you married then? Where did you live that interests them? What are the names of relatives they know? etc.).

A great way to share spiritual legacy stories is at bedtime for your children, grandchildren, or other children. Be prepared ahead of time with specific little spiritual legacy stories that you can tell them when you tuck them in at night. You are sowing life into them.

How sophisticated should you be?

If you write a story, how sophisticated should your writing or story telling be? Write at a sixth-grade level at the most. That's what newspapers used to do. If you use difficult words, define them.

Remember, if you are seeking recognition by telling the story, the spiritual legacy won't have anointing. If, on the other hand, you are sharing the spiritual legacy of God in your life, it will have power.

Add context to the story

Think in terms of events of the day or the time period in which the story happened in order to give it more context and to help the future generation get a little historical perspective.

If you describe an historical event/circumstance/period or a term or condition from the past that they may not understand, explain it in a sentence or two. This just adds some nice color to the story. For example, you may describe hippies, the Vietnam War, Watergate, Elvis, the Charismatic movement, or many other events that could add some color. Describe a little how people looked, how they acted, what their attitudes were during the time period of the story.

The self-contained story structure

You are just telling a story, a short example of something that illustrates God's faithfulness. You can do it in three easy steps.

1. Start with an attention grabber, something that makes them want to hear, read, or watch more.

    • "I never thought such a small decision could impact the rest of my life so dramatically. But God did."

    • "When I got up that morning, I had no idea this day would be like no other day in my life."

    • "Sometimes being a parent isn't all it's cracked up to be."

2. Tell the story.

    • Keep on the main track and don't bring in a lot of other stuff. You don't want to lose the message in all your verbiage.

    • Include details that would be of interest to your audience. For example, if you are creating this legacy for your children, tell them something about where you (and possibly your spouse) were living at the time or something else that would hold their attention and add a little color to the story.

    • Remember, you are not preaching to them. You are telling a story. Don't tell them what to do.

    • You don't have to quote a lot of the Bible, although you should feel free to add a relevant verse or two that contributes to the story. As the apostle Paul says, "You are the living letter." Simply let them read you.

3. Have a conclusion that wraps up the story.

- "I discovered that God is even concerned about my small decisions."
- "I never know what a new day will bring. So, I prepare for each day by having a conversation with the Father when I first get up."

MAKING YOUR SPIRITUAL LEGACY STORIES PERMANENT

"And there are also many other things that Jesus did, which if they were written one by one, I suppose that even the world itself could not contain the books that would be written. Amen." (Jn 21:25)

Choose a medium (don't panic; that's the singular for media) for your story

Are you going to tell it to someone directly? Are you going to record it so someone can listen to it later? Are you going to video it so they can watch it (perhaps putting it on YouTube)?

Let's look at each option.

Writing your story

Many 50+ers want to write a book or create a family history. I already talked about the "self-contained" story structure. You can use this format to make many spiritual legacy stories.

The next question is how to capture the information. In a previous chapter I gave you many ideas for spiritual legacy stories. Now let's talk about how to write down the stories.

You don't have to be a writer in order to write a spiritual legacy story. Just speak the story out and write down what you speak. And don't worry about spelling and grammar either. You can always get someone to clean up your spelling. Your children or grandchildren or someone else who would be interested in what you are doing could be a great choice to help you with a few grammar details. The main thing is the story itself. Don't fret over the rest.

One of the easiest ways to capture all the stories is to write all the stories in one document in Microsoft Word. Word allows you to make a table of contents so you know where each story is within the longer document.

Making a table of contents--

If you don't understand the directions below, simply get someone who knows Microsoft Word to help you. There are many versions of Microsoft Word. For your version you may have to click on the Help pull down menu and type in the search box: "how to create the table of contents." Once you have created a table of contents, you'll love it.

In order to create a table of content, you must first make a title (heading 1) for each story when you type it.

1. Make the first page of your document a blank page so you can insert the table of contents later.

2. Type some stories and give each story a title.
   a. Think of your possible title and type it.
   b. Next, highlight the title by dragging the curser over it.

c. Then click on "Heading 1" found in the "Styles" box above what you are typing. The typing will turn into a headline. Below is an example of what the Styles box may look like. Simply click on "Heading 1," and what you highlighted will be a headline.

Styles			
AaBbCcDdEɛ	AaBbCcDdEɛ	AaBbCcDɛ	AaBbCcDdEɛ
Normal	No Spacing	Heading 1	Heading 2

3. At the end of each story, you should insert a page break. That way each new story will start on a new page. Simply put your curser at the end of the story. Click on the "Insert" tab at the top of the page and choose "break" and then choose "page break" if your version of Word is set up that way.

4. You also want to add page numbers to the bottom of your pages. Even if you don't add page numbers, you will see the correct pages in the table of contents after you create the table of contents. You can again probably click on the "Insert" tab at the top of your document screen and then select "page numbers." Page numbers will automatically appear at the bottom of each page.

5. Now it's time to create a wonderful table of contents so you can keep track of what you are writing.

a. Go back to the very first page of your document that you made a blank page and click your curser at the top of the page.

b. If you are typing on a PC, select the "References"

tab on the Word menu and click on Table of Contents. (On Microsoft Word for Mac, the T of C may be found by clicking on the "Document Elements" tab.)

And, bingo, you have a Table of Contents.

(Notice that the Heading 1 style is the first heading. Whatever you create in the Heading 2 style is the first indent. Whatever you type using Heading 3 is the next indent.)

After you type more stories, you will want to update your table of contents to show the new stories. Click on the Table of Contents. Then choose "Update Table" from the References tab. Notice in the above picture example that you can see "Update Table".

If you don't understand all this, just go to the Help menu in your version of Microsoft Word and ask "How to create a table of contents" or "How to update a table of contents."

How to publish your story

Well, there are many ways to publish your story, depending on how good you are at writing or typing, who might help you, how much time you have to put into the story, and so on. Below are some suggestions for ways to publish your story.

Some 50+ers want to create a book about their life's experiences. That is fine. Consider who your audience will be. That will largely determine how you are going to publish what you've written.

Are you writing to family members and future generations of your family? You have some easy options here.

After you have had a friend clean up your spelling errors, you can simply print out your document with its Table of Contents included. Then make yourself a cover page. You can go to a quick print store and have your manuscript printed and bound.

You can add a few photos to the above example and have them as part of your stories also in this "memories book."

Many people are interested in **creating a family history**. You can use the spiritual legacy stories as part of this family history. If you are doing a family history, you may want to do it chronologically. (I have an example of thinking through that process as one of the exercises in the "Creating a Spiritual Legacy" chapter.) Family histories are good when they also include photos. You can be very simple in doing this, such as my suggestion above about adding some photos to your manuscript. Or you can be much more professional.

If you are up to the task and understand computers pretty well, you should look into **www.blurb.com**. Blurb has templates that allow you to place your writing in a book and also add photos. You will download their software in order to create your book. I created a sample family legacy book using Blurb's software, and was very satisfied. You can create a cover. You can choose the trim size for the book. You can determine if you want it to be printed in color or black and white. You can then print only the number of books you need. I know some 50+ers who are considering creating a spiritual legacy family history as Christmas presents for their grandkids.

You can even publish your book as an e-book if your grandkids want to read and see it on their computers instead of in printed form.

Blurb isn't ideal because it focuses on photos, but it does have nice ability to place your writing into the document. Shutterfly (**www.shutterfly.com**) is another well-known company that creates photo books. However, it is very difficult get your writing into the book because the writing does not automatically flow into the pages. Blurb is much better in my opinion for combining stories with photos.

Here are a few considerations when creating a spiritual legacy family history

» You will want a logical arrangement of the material. Is it going to be arranged based on the big events or highlights of your life? Is it going to be strictly chronological? Is it going to be based on each side of the family?

» Notice that I called this a "spiritual legacy family history." It seems everyone wants to know where they came from and who their ancestors were. You will want to include that information. Photos are good for giving a pictorial representation. However, you will also want to share some stories of God's faithfulness and provision in your life so that future generations know how to live in God's love and purpose. You already have their attention with the history; let the spiritual legacy stories speak to their hearts.

» Don't preach when you tell the spiritual legacy stories. You are the living letter that they are reading. Simply tell what happened.

» Add photos that are appropriate for the time period. Be sure to write captions so that the readers know who is in the picture, what was happening in the picture, and when the picture took place.

If you are thinking of publishing your story for the world to see, i.e., publishing a book, you have to take an entirely different approach. Unless you have a powerful story that is unique and could attract a large audience, you may not want to pursue publishing a book. I was the editor of a Christian book publishing company. Most of the manuscripts I received had some good ideas, even God-inspired ideas. But we wouldn't publish them because we knew the audience would be too small. Or we realized that the ideas in the book were meant more for the person writing the book than for a larger audience.

Of course the world has changed with the advent of self publishing. So you can actually self publish a book using **www.amazon.com** or **www.lulu.com**. You can order the number of books you think you can sell, and they can also make the books available for purchase.

If you are considering publishing a book, here are a few considerations:

> » What is your motivation? If your motivation is to be recognized or appreciated, then you have the wrong motive. Many Christians won't admit that this is what is driving them to want to publish a book, but if they examine their hearts, they might find out differently.
> » Many people have had supernatural experiences and revelations. That is what God does. Just because you have had miracles and supernatural encounters doesn't mean it will sell in book form. However, as spiritual legacies, these stories have profound impact!!
> » Is the truth you discovered to be shared with others, or was the LORD teaching you something for your own life and purpose?

Recording or videoing your spiritual legacy stories

Writing is more formal than speaking. When you tell a story to someone, you are relaxed.

Recording—

With the advent of smart phones, you have a recording device with you all the time. You simply have to record something and then email that recording to someone else. Wow. This is great for telling spiritual legacy stories to grandkids. You can surprise them with a funny story of something that happened to you. You can tell them how God first got your attention or how God led you to your mate or what you thought when you became a father or mother. You can tell a thousand stories. And your grandchildren will listen.

The good news about recording is that you can plan it out ahead. Review the "self-contained story structure" from earlier in the Appendix. Take a few brief notes if you want so that you remember the details. Then tell the story and email it to your grandchildren.

Videoing—

Videoing your individual spiritual legacy stories is a powerful way to share God's faithfulness with future generations. Video is the preferred entertainment and communication form of the younger generations. So you are actually communicating with them in ways they understand--which is very important.

In addition, they get to see your face. And they will see the authentic emotions connected to the spiritual legacy story itself.

And it is so easy for them to watch the videos because you can put them on YouTube or on Facebook, two main social media repositories that almost all younger generation types visit regularly. (They might even think you are hip or cool, if they only knew what those words mean.)

Again you can use your smart phone video camera and publish on, say, YouTube. Or you can buy an inexpensive digital video camera that costs less than $200. These cameras even come with editing software and allow you to post what you recorded to YouTube and Facebook.

You can also use a video editing program on your computer. I use iMovie, which came with my Macintosh computer. I have also used other video editing programs. To edit a video spiritual legacy is easy. And when you do it, you can also add a title and put other information on the video if you want. But I recommend keeping it simple, keeping it you, keeping the beauty of your story the main event as you relax and tell the story. Don't be afraid of emotions, either. I have videoed spiritual legacy stories from many 50+ers. And when they describe the LORD's hand in their lives, they are often deeply moved themselves.

It is very easy for you to get a YouTube account. Simply set up a gmail account. Then you can create a YouTube account. When you learn how to put your spiritual legacy stories on YouTube, you can make them unlisted, and only those you send the link to can see them. Or you can make them public, and anyone can see them. You can share your spiritual legacy stories with the world if you want.

The 50+ Blessing Generation group at MorningStar Fellowship Church in Fort Mill, SC, have recorded spiritual legacies and put them on YouTube. Go to www.YouTube. com and type in spirituallegacy (no spaces between the words) in the search field. Or you can go to **http://www. youtube.com/user/SpiritualLegacy** to view the spiritual legacies.

Putting your spiritual legacy stories on your own YouTube channel will allow others to see them for years to come if you want. It is a great way to honestly share spiritual legacy stories.

You are the Joshua and Caleb generation. Future generations need to know of God's faithfulness, love, and provision. You will make a difference in their lives.